D1535169

TRIBUTE TO

FREUD

BY H. D.

With unpublished letters
by Freud to the author

PANTHEON

To Sigmund Freud

ἀμύμων ἰητήρ

"blameless physician"

FOREWORD

TRUTH is stranger than fiction. This book is strange in the way that truth is when it is complicated and delicately told. It is an account of one woman's psychoanalysis as reported by her. She is one of the greatest living poets. She was 47 years old when she began her analysis with Freud. He was 77. The physical scene is shifted from Vienna to London when Freud goes there, but the fantasy ranges from ancient Egypt to eternity. The two main characters are Freud himself, and H. D., the poet and dreamer, supported by a large and various cast who enter and leave the scene by the richest of associational doors.

It is at once more and less than an account of a psychoanalysis. It does not aim at conscientious historical coverage of the material revealed but rather it is a poetic document in its own right. If the word "psychoanalysis" were not mentioned, if the name "Freud" were deleted everywhere it appears, and replaced by the words "superior being," the document would still contain its unique power and rhythm. Although it is written in so-called prose it has the effect of a long dramatic poem.

When H. D. first published this work in an English magazine, it carried the title "Writing on the Wall." The title crystallizes a vast content in a few words. Its meaning will be different for each individual but this is part of what it means to me: the wall is Reality, the artist is the Creator, creating is projecting, the artist (or dreamer) creates by projecting what is in his or her mind onto the wall of reality which is the wall of the world. H. D. has documented her own writing on the wall in this record far better than it could have been done by any electronic recording device. Here is an aspect of analysis vividly and consistently presented; many of the problems familiar to analyst and analysand are touched on here but with the fresh excitement of the poet. The transference in all its glory stands unveiled. We see H. D.'s idea of the counter-transference, the patient who came before, the patient who came after, what one senses of another, the odor of the analytic neurosis. All these sights and smells and feelings are rendered as vividly as if one entered a busy kitchen where a great banquet was being prepared—pots here, pans there, all filled with the meats and vegetables

For a dictionary of sublime irrelevances.

of everyday life, only somehow here concocted with the rare spices and the rich sauces of the poet-analysand and the magician-analyst. Freud in his way was a poet, and it is as a poet that H. D. reports him by the same steps that he became known to her.

With literary magic H. D. has re-created step by step her experience as analysand, and she has done it all so gracefully and so perceptively that one can rejoice that one more facet of analytic experience in general and Freud in particular has thus been unwrapped from the sinister and grotesque swaddling clothes in which laymen have dressed it.

This book thus celebrates the meaningfulness of human individuality. It is a poem or a poetic prose entity, a dramatized integrated unique message and a communication of one spirit to another. It breathes the atmosphere of collaboration not only of the self with other selves but of the selves within the self. Never have I seen sentiments so subtly conveyed or so microscopically catalogued, not even in the writings of Freud himself, master dialectician that he was.

MERRILL MOORE

IT WAS VIENNA, 1933–1934. I had a room in
the Hotel Regina, Freiheitsplatz. I had a
small calendar on my table. I counted the
days and marked them off, calculating the
weeks. My sessions were limited, time went
so quickly. As I stopped to leave my key at
the desk, the hall porter said, "Some day,
will you remember me to the Professor?" I
said I would if the opportunity arose. He
said, "—and ah, the Frau Professor! There
is a wonderful lady." I said I had not met
the Frau Professor but had heard that she
was the perfect wife for him and there
couldn't be—could there?—a greater possible compliment. The porter said, "You
know Berggasse? After the—well, later
when the Professor is no longer with us,
they will name it Freudgasse." I went down
Berggasse, turned in the familiar entrance;
Berggasse 19, Wien IX, it was. There were
wide stone steps and a balustrade. Sometimes I met someone else coming down.

The stone staircase was curved. There

were two doors on the landing. The one to the right was the Professor's professional door; the one to the left, the Freud family door. Apparently, the two apartments had been arranged so that there should be as little confusion as possible between family and patients or students; there was the Professor who belonged to us, there was the Professor who belonged to the family; it was a large family with ramifications, in-laws, distant relatives, family friends. There were other apartments above but I did not very often pass anyone on the stairs, except the analysand whose hour preceded mine.

My hours or sessions had been arranged for me, four days a week from five to six; one day, from twelve to one. At least, that was the arrangement for the second series of sessions which, I have noted, began the end of October, 1934. I left a number of books and letters in Switzerland when I left there, actually after the war had begun; among them was my 1933 Vienna diary. I am under the impression that the Professor had arranged the second series to accord with the first, as I had often said to him that that near-evening hour was almost my favourite of the whole day. Anyhow, I had five weeks then. The last session was December 1, 1934. The first series began in

March, 1933 and lasted somewhat longer, between three and four months. I had not planned coming back to Vienna, but a great deal had happened between the summer of 1933 and the autumn of 1934. I had heard the news of the Dollfuss affair with some anxiety, but that had not caused any personal repercussions. I came back to Vienna because I heard about the man I sometimes met, coming down the stairs. He had been lecturing at a conference in Johannesburg. He flew his own plane there. On the way back, he crashed in Tanganyika.

2

I DID NOT always pass him on the stairs. He might be lingering on, prolonging his talk in the Professor's study or consulting room, in which case, after hanging up my coat in the hall, I might miss him. I would be ushered direct into the waiting room. Or it might happen that my predecessor emerged from the Professor's sanctum at the same time that I was about to enter. He would be reaching for his coat or his hat while I was disposing of mine. He was very tall, he looked English—yet English with a catch. He had, it later appeared, spent some time at Oxford, before or after receiving his Continental degree—in any case, he was not German, not American; but how does one know these things? He was, as it happened, exactly what I thought him, "English with a catch," in fact, a Dutchman.

I did not know that his name was J. J. van der Leeuw until afterwards. Once he spoke to me at the Professor's bidding, about exchanging hours. That was a summer day in the big house outside the town, at Döbling, where the family moved for the hot months. It would have been a day late in June, or early July, 1933. The arrangement for receiving us there was more informal, and one did not have quite the same sense of authenticity or *reality* as in the Professor's own home. However, I did not say good-bye to Vienna in the house of a stranger on its outskirts. I came back.

I told the Professor why I had come back. The Professor was 77 at the time of our first sessions. I was 47. Dr. van der Leeuw was considerably younger. He was known among them, the Professor told me, as the Flying Dutchman. He was an eminent scholar. He had come officially to study with the Professor with the idea of the application of the principles of psycho-analysis to general education, with the greater practical aim of international co-operation and understanding. He was wealthy, influential, well-born. He owned vast plantations in the Dutch East Indies and had travelled in India for the purpose of occult investigation. He had contacted a teacher or young devotee there, had been influenced by the Eastern teaching, but that had not satisfied him. He wanted to apply the laws of spiritual being to the acute problems of to-day. It seemed to me that he was the perfect man for the perfect job. The Professor had not told me that J. J. van der Leeuw was himself aware of a deeply rooted desire or subconscious tendency connected with his brilliant avi-ation. The Flying Dutchman knew that at any given moment, in the air—his element —he was likely to fly too high, to fly too quickly. "That was really what concerned me," said the Professor. "I can tell you now that that was really what concerned us both." The Professor added, "After he left, last time, I felt I had found the solu-tion, I really had the answer. But it was too late."

I said to the Professor, "I always had a feeling of satisfaction, of security when I passed Dr. van der Leeuw on the stairs or saw him in the hall. He seemed so self-sufficient, so poised—and you had told me about his work. I felt all the time that he was the person who would apply, carry on the torch—carry on your ideas, but not in a stereotyped way. I felt that you and your work and the future of your work were especially bequeathed to him. Oh, I know there is the great body of the Psycho-Analytical Association, research workers, doctors, trained analysts and so on! But Dr. van der Leeuw was different. I know that you have felt this very deeply. I came back to Vienna to tell you how sorry I am."

The Professor said, "You have come to take his place."

Bang!

3

I DID NOT consciously think about the Flying Dutchman or connect him with my own work or weave him into my reveries. My own problems, my own intense, dynamic interest in the unfolding of the unconscious or the subconscious pattern, did not seem to include him. He was so personable, so presentable, apparently so richly intellectually and materially endowed. I envied him, I think, his apparently uncomplicated personality. He was an intellectual type but externalized, the diplomatic or even business type; one did not think of him as tortured or troubled; there seemed nothing of *Sturm und Drang* about him. He appeared scholarly, yes, but not in a bookish introverted sense. You would have said that his body fitted him as perfectly and as suavely as the grey or blue cloth that covered it; his soul fitted his body, you would have said, and his mind fitted his brain or his head; the forehead was high, unfurrowed; his eyes looked perceptive with a mariner's blue gaze; the eyes were a shade off or a shade above blue-grey yet with that grey North Sea in them. Yes— cool, cold, perceptive yet untroubled, you would have said. When later I came to think of it, yes, then it did seem that he was mercurial, Mercury.

I do not think that the name of the winged messenger, Hermes of the Greeks, Mercury of the Romans, ever came up in my talks with the Professor, except once in a roundabout way when I had a dream sequence that included a figure from the famous Raphael Donner fountain in the Marktplatz. This is a very beautiful fountain with reclining figures of river gods, two women and two men. My dream was connected with a young man of my acquaintance in London; his name is not Brooks but his name does suggest streams and rivers so we may call him Brooks. I connected this young Mr. Brooks with the figure of the younger of the male river gods in my dream sequence. It was then that I said to the Professor that the reclining bronze fountain figure had certain affinities with the poised Bolognese Mercury. We agreed that the Raphael Donner figure was the more attractive and original of the two, but that if you should raise the reclining river god and stand him on his feet, he might faintly resemble the Mercury—or in reverse, set the Mercury down to lean on his elbow and he might almost take the place of the bronze fountain figure. It was in any case our Professor's charming way to fall in with an idea, to do it justice but not to overstress unimportant details. For this seemed unimportant at the time.

Perhaps it is not very important now. It is interesting, however, to note in retrospect how the mind hedges away. I connected the Raphael Donner figure, and by implication the Mercury, with a charming but not very important young London acquaintance, while the actual personable image is there in Vienna and was there—had been there—reclining on this very couch, every hour just before my own session. As I say, I did not consciously think about Dr. van der Leeuw or weave him into my reveries. Nor did I think of him as Mercury, the Messenger of the Gods and the Leader of the Dead, after he crashed.

He was a stranger. I did not really know him. We had spoken once in the house at Döbling, outside Vienna. The Professor waved him across the large, unfamiliar drawing room. Dr. van der Leeuw bowed, he addressed me in polite, distinguished German, would the *gnädige Frau* object to altering her hour for one day, to-morrow? I answered him in English, I would not mind at all, I would come at 4, he at 5. He thanked me pleasantly in friendly English, without a trace of accent. That was the first and last time I spoke to the Flying Dutchman. We had exchanged "hours."

THE PROFESSOR WAS 77. His birthday in
May was significant. The consulting room
in the strange house contained some of his
treasures and his famous desk. The room
looked the same, except for the desk. In-
stead of the semicircle of priceless little *ob-
jets d'art*, there was a carefully arranged
series of vases; each contained a spray of
orchids or a single flower. I had nothing
for the Professor. I said, "I am sorry, I
haven't brought you anything because I
couldn't find what I wanted." I said,
"Anyway, I wanted to give you something different." My remark might have
seemed a shade careless, a shade arrogant.
It might have seemed either of these things,
or both. I do not know how the Professor
translated it. He waved me to the couch,
satisfied or unsatisfied with my apparently
casual regard for his birthday.

I had not found what I wanted so I did
not give him anything. In one of our talks
in the old room at Berggasse, we had gone
off on one of our journeys. Sometimes, the
Professor knew actually my terrain, sometimes it was implicit in a statue or a picture,
like that old-fashioned steel engraving of
the Temple at Karnak that hung above the

couch. I had visited that particular temple, he had not. But this time it was Italy; we were together in Rome. The years went forward, then backward. The shuttle of the years ran a thread that wove my pattern into the Professor's. "Ah, the Spanish Steps," said the Professor. "It was those branches of almond," I said; "of all the flowers and the flower baskets, I remember those best." "But," said the Professor, "the gardenias! In Rome, even *I* could afford to wear a gardenia." It was not that he conjured up the past and invoked the future. It was a present that was in the past or a past that was in the future.

Even I could search Vienna for a single gardenia or a cluster of gardenias. But I could not find them. Another year, I wrote from London, asking a friend in Vienna—an English student there—to make a special effort to find a cluster of gardenias for the Professor's birthday. She wrote back, "I looked everywhere for the gardenias. But the florists told me that Professor Freud liked orchids and that people always ordered orchids for his birthday; they thought you would like to know. I sent the orchids for you."

IT WAS SOMETIME later that the Professor received my gardenias. It was not a birthday, it was not Vienna. I had been to see him in London, in new surroundings. He had arrived lately, an exile. It was a large house with a garden. There had been much discussion and anxiety concerning the Professor's famous collection of Greek and Egyptian antiquities and the various Chinese and other Oriental treasures. The boxes had at last arrived, although the family expressed some doubt as to whether or not the entire treasure-trove, or even any of it, would be found intact. At least, the boxes had come, due to the influence and generosity of the Professor's friend and disciple, Madame Marie Bonaparte, the Princess George of Greece; "the Princess" or "our Princess," the Professor called her. I had expressed surprise at seeing several Greek figures on his desk. It seemed to be the same desk in a room that suggested that summer room in the house outside Vienna of my first visit in 1933. But this was autumn, 1938. "How did you manage to bring those from Vienna?" I asked him. "I did not bring them," he said. "The Princess had them waiting for me in Paris, so that I should feel at home there." It was a treacherous, evil world but there was yet loyalty and beauty in it. It had been a flying, frightening journey. He had told me, five years before in Vienna, that travelling was even then out of the question for him. It was distinctly forbidden him by the distinguished specialist who was always within beck and call. (If I am not mistaken, this devoted friend accompanied the Professor on his journey across the Continent.) It was difficult, seeing the familiar desk, the familiar new-old images on the desk there, to realize that this was London. Indeed, it was better to think of it in terms of a temporary slightly familiar dwelling, as that summer house at Döbling. This pleasant district was geographically, in a sense, to London, what Döbling had been to Vienna. But there was no return to Berggasse, Freudgasse that was to have been.

6

BUT IN IMAGINATION at least, in the mist of a late afternoon, I could still continue a quest, a search. There might be gardenias somewhere. I found them in a West End florist's and scribbled on a card, "to greet the return of the Gods." The gardenias reached the Professor. I have his letter.

20 Maresfield Gardens,
London, N.W. 3
Nov. 28th, 1938

Dear H. D.,

I got to-day some flowers. By chance or intention they are my favourite flowers, those I most admire. Some words "to greet the return of the Gods" (other people read: Goods). No name. I suspect you to be responsible for the gift. If I have guessed right don't answer but accept my hearty thanks for so charming a gesture. In any case,

affectionately yours,
Sigm. Freud

7

I ONLY SAW the Professor once more. It was summer again. French windows opened on a pleasant stretch of lawn. The Gods or the Goods were suitably arranged on ordered shelves. I was not alone with the Professor. He sat quiet, a little wistful it seemed, withdrawn. I was afraid then, as I had often been afraid, of impinging, disturbing his detachment, of draining his vitality. I had no choice in the matter, anyway. There were others present and the conversation was carried on in an ordered, conventional manner. Like the Gods or the Goods, we were seated in a pleasant circle; a conventionally correct yet superficially sustained ordered hospitality prevailed. There was a sense of outer security, at least no words were spoken to recall a devastatingly near past or to evoke an equivocal future. I was in Switzerland when soon after the announcement of a World at War the official London news bulletin announced that Dr. Sigmund Freud, who had opened up the field of the knowledge of the unconscious mind, the innovator or founder of the science of psychoanalysis, was dead.

8

I HAD ORIGINALLY written *had gone*, but I crossed it out deliberately. Yes, he was dead. I was not emotionally involved. The Professor was an old man. He was 83. The *– 1939* war was on us. I did not grieve for the Professor or think of him. He was spared so much. He had confined his researches to the living texture of wholesome as well as unwholesome thought, but contemporary thought, you might say. That is to say, he had brought the past into the present with his *the childhood of the individual is the childhood of the race*—or is it the other way round?—*the childhood of the race is the childhood of the individual*. In any case (whether or not, the converse also is true), he had opened up, among others, that particular field of the unconscious mind that went to prove that the traits and tendencies of obscure aboriginal tribes, as well as the shape and substance of the rituals of vanished civilizations, were still inherent in the human mind—the human psyche, if you will. But according to his theories the soul existed explicitly, or showed its form and shape in and through the medium of the mind, and the body, as affected by the mind's ecstasies or disorders. About the greater transcendental issues, we never argued. But there was an argument implicit in our very bones. We had come together in order to substantiate something. I did not know what. There was something that was beating in my brain; I do not say my heart—my brain. I wanted it to be let out. I wanted to free myself of repetitive thoughts and experiences—my own and those of many of my contemporaries. I did not specifically realize just what it was I wanted, but I knew that I, like most of the people I knew, in England, America and on the Continent of Europe, were drifting. We were drifting. Where? I did not know but at least I accepted the fact that we *were* drifting. At least, I knew this—I would (before the current of inevitable events swept me right into the main stream and so on to the cataract) stand aside, if I could (if it were not already too late), and take stock of my possessions. You might say that I had—yes, I had something that I specifically owned. I *owned* myself. I did not really, of course. My family, my friends and my circumstances owned me. But I *had* something. Say it was a narrow birch-bark canoe. The great forest of the unknown, the supernormal or supernatural, was all around and about us. With the current gathering force, I could at least pull in to the shallows before it was too late, take stock of my very modest possessions of mind and body, and ask the old Hermit who lived on the edge of this vast domain to talk to me, to tell me, if he would, how best to steer my course.

We touched lightly on some of the more abstruse transcendental problems, it is true, but we related them to the familiar family-complex. Tendencies of thought and imagination, however, were not cut away, were not pruned even. My imagination wandered at will; my dreams were revealing, and many of them drew on classical or Biblical symbolism. Thoughts were things, to be collected, collated, analysed, shelved or resolved. Fragmentary ideas, apparently unrelated, were often found to be part of a special layer or stratum of thought and memory, therefore to belong together; these were sometimes skilfully pieced together like the exquisite Greek tear-jars and iridescent glass bowls and vases that gleamed in the dusk from the shelves of the cabinet that faced me where I stretched, propped up on the couch in the room in Berggasse 19, Wien IX. The dead were living in so far as they lived in memory or were recalled in dream.

9

In any case, affectionately yours . . . I did not know what enraged him suddenly. I veered round off the couch, my feet on the floor. I do not know exactly what I had said. I have certain notes that I jotted down while in Vienna, but I never worked them over and have barely glanced at them since. I do not want to become involved in the strictly historical sequence. I wish to re-call the impressions, or rather I wish the impressions to recall me. Let the impressions come in their own way, make their own sequence. "There will be plenty of memoirs about the Professor," Walter Schmideberg said to me. "I expect Sachs and the Princess have already done theirs."

The analyst Schmideberg spoke ironi-cally; he was a young Austrian officer on the Russian front, in the first World War, a "captain of horses" as he described him-self to me in the earlier days before his English had become so set. "Captain of horses" conveyed more to me than "cav-alry officer" or "officer of the guards"; just as "needle-tree," to which he referred one day, than "pine" or even "evergreen." So the impact of a language, as well as the im-pact of an impression may become "correct," become "stylized," lose its living quality. It is easy to be caught, like Schmideberg, in the noose of self-criticism, it is easy to say, "Everybody will be scribbling memoirs," but the answer to that is, "Indeed yes, but neither the Princess George of Greece nor Dr. Hanns Sachs aforetime of Vienna and Berlin, later of Boston, Massachusetts, can scribble exactly *my* impressions of the Professor." Moreover, I don't think anyone could give us a more tender, humorous account of the Professor (if he would let the impressions carry him out of himself) than the former young Rittmeister Schmideberg, who became the world's adept at smuggling cigars to Berggasse during the darkest days of that war, and with whom the Professor kept faith during his bitter year of confinement in an Italian prison-camp, ironically after the war had ended.

IO

SO MUCH FOR the Princess, Hanns Sachs and Walter Schmideberg, the one-time Rittmeister of the 15th Imperial Austro-Hungarian Hussars of His Royal Highness,

Archduke Francis Salvator. For myself, I veer round, uncanonically seated stark upright with my feet on the floor. The Professor himself is uncanonical enough; he is beating with his hand, with his fist, on the head-piece of the old-fashioned horsehair sofa that had heard more secrets than the confession box of any popular Roman Catholic father-confessor in his heyday. This was the homely historical instrument of the original scheme of psychotherapy, of psychoanalysis, the science of the unravelling of the tangled skeins of the unconscious mind and the healing implicit in the process. *Consciously*, I was not aware of having said anything that might account for the Professor's outburst. And even as I veered around, facing him, my mind was detached enough to wonder if this was some idea of *his* for speeding up the analytic content or redirecting the flow of associated images. The Professor said, "The trouble is—I am an old man—*you do not think it worth your while to love me.*"

II

THE IMPACT of his words was too dreadful—I simply felt nothing at all. I said nothing. What did he expect me to say? Exactly it was as if the Supreme Being had
hammered with his fist on the back of the
couch where I had been lying. Why, anyway, did he do that? He must know every-
thing or he didn't know anything. He must
know what I felt. Maybe he did, maybe
that was what this was all about. Maybe,
anyway, it was just a trick, something to
shock me, to break something in myself of
which I was partially aware—something
that would not, must not be broken. I was
here because I must not be broken. If I
were broken, I could not go on here with
the Professor. Did he think it was easy to
leave friendly, comfortable surroundings
and come to a strange city, to beard him,
himself, the dragon, in his very den? Vienna? Venice? My mother had come here
on her honeymoon, tired, having "done"
Italy as a bride. Maybe my mother was already sheltering the child, a girl, that first
child that lived such a very short time. It
was the bread she talked of, Vienna and
how she loved the different rolls and the
shapes of them and ones with poppy-seeds

and Oh—the coffee! Why had I come to Vienna? The Professor had said in the very beginning that I had come to Vienna hoping to find my mother. Mother? Mamma. But my mother was dead. I was dead; that is, the child in me that had called her mamma was dead. Anyhow, he was a terribly frightening old man, too old and too detached, too wise and too famous altogether, to beat that way with his fist, like a child hammering a porridge-spoon on the table.

I slid back onto the couch. You might say I sneaked back. With due deliberation and the utmost savoir faire, I rearranged the rug that had slid to the floor. The couch was slippery, the head-piece at the back was hard. I was almost too long; if I were a little longer my feet would touch the old-fashioned porcelain stove that stood edge-wise in the corner. *The Nürnberg Stove* was a book that my mother had liked. I could not remember a single incident of the book and would not take the time to go through all the intricacies of explaining to the Professor that I was thinking of a book called *The Nürnberg Stove*. It was all very obvious; there was the stove, throwing out its pleasantly perceptible glow, there was the stove itself in the corner. I saw the porcelain stove and I thought of a book called *The Nürnberg Stove*, but why take up time going into all that, anyway?

There was the stove, but there were moments when one felt a little chilly. I smoothed the folds of the rug, I glanced surreptitiously at my wrist-watch. The other day the Professor had reproached me for jerking out my arm and looking at my watch. He had said, "I keep an eye on the time—I will tell you when the session is over. You need not keep looking at the time, as if you were in a hurry to get away." I fingered the strap of my watch, I tucked my cold hands under the rug. I always found the rug carefully folded at the foot of the couch when I came in. Did the little maid Paula come in from the hall and fold the rug or did the preceding analysand fold it, as I always carefully did before leaving? I was preceded by the Flying Dutchman; he probably left the rug just anyhow—a man would. Should I ask the Professor if everybody folded the rug on leaving, or if only I did this? The Professor had said in the beginning that he classed me in the same category as the Flying Dutchman—we were students. I was a student, working under the direction of the greatest mind of this and of perhaps many succeeding generations. But the Professor was not always right.

12

I DID NOT argue with the Professor. In fact, as I say, I did not have the answer. If he expected to rouse me to some protestation of affection, he did not then succeed in doing so—the root or the current ran too deep. One day he said, "*To-day we have tunnelled very deep.*" One day he said, "I struck oil. It was I who struck oil. But the contents of the oil wells have only just been sampled. There is oil enough, material enough for research and exploitation, to last 50 years, to last 100 years—or longer." He said, "My discoveries are not primarily a heal-all. My discoveries are a basis for a very grave philosophy. There are very few who understand this, *there are very few who are capable of understanding this.*" One day he said to me, "You discovered for yourself what I discovered for the race." To all that, I will hope to return later. At the moment, I am lying on the couch. I have just readjusted the rug that had slipped to the floor. I have tucked my hands under the rug. I am wondering if the Professor caught me looking at my wrist-watch. I am really somewhat shattered. But there is no answering flare-back.

13

THERE IS the old-fashioned porcelain stove at the foot of the couch. My father had a stove of that sort in the outdoor office or study he had had built in the garden of my first home. There was a couch there, too, and a rug folded at the foot. It too had a slightly elevated head-piece. My father's study was lined with books, as this room was. There was a smell of leather, the crackling of wood in the stove, as here. There was one picture, a photograph of Rembrandt's Dissection, and a skull on the top of my father's highest set of shelves. There was a white owl under a bell-jar. I could sit on the floor with a doll or a folder of paper dolls, but I must not speak to him when he was writing at his table. What he was "writing" was rows and rows of num-bers, but I could then scarcely distinguish the shape of a number from a letter, or know which was which. I must not speak to my father when he lay stretched out on the couch, because he worked at night and so must not be disturbed when he lay down on the couch and closed his eyes by day. But now it is I who am lying on the couch in the room lined with books.

But no, there are not many books in this room; it is the other room that is lined with books. The window in this room and the one in the other room look out on to a courtyard, I believe. I am not sure of this. It is quiet here, anyway. There is no sound of traffic from the street, no familiar household sounds as from the Freud-family side of the house. We are quite alone here in this room. But there are two rooms really, though the room beyond is almost part of this room with the wide-parted double doors. There is dusk and darkness beyond, through the parted double doors to the right of the stove, as I lie here. There is the door across the room that opens in from the little waiting room. There is the other door, at right angles, the exit door. It leads through a rather dark passage or a little room that suggests a pantry or laboratory. Then there is the hall beyond it, where we hang our coats on pegs that somehow suggest school or college. The Flying Dutchman has been and gone. Not only are we alike in our relation to the Professor, as seekers or "students" as he calls us, but we bear the same relation to the couch that I am lying on. When, in the beginning, I expressed a slight embarrassment at being "almost too tall," the Professor put me at ease by saying that the analysand who preceded me was "actually considerably taller."

14

MY BROTHER is considerably taller. I am 5 and he is 7, or I am 3 and he is 5. It is summer. The grass is somewhat dry, a few leaves crackle under our feet. They have fallen from a pear tree that has large russet pears. The pears have been gathered. (*Pears? Pairs?*) There is a tree opposite this, that has small yellow pears; they ripen earlier. The tree next our tree is a crab-apple tree and there is a slice of a large log under it. The log is like a round table or a solid thick stool. It is too heavy for us to move, but Eric, our half-brother (a grown man to us), shifted it easily. We saw what was under the heavy immovable log. There was a variety of entertaining exhibits; small things like ants moved very quickly; they raced frantically around but always returned to the same ridge of damp earth or tiny lump of loam. In neatly sliced runnels, some white, wingless creatures lay curled. The base of the log had been the roof of a series of little pockets or neat open graves, rather like Aztec or Egyptian burial-chambers, but I did not know that. These curled, white slugs were unborn things. They were repulsive enough, like unlanced boils. Or it is possible that they were not essentially repulsive—they might be cocoonless larvae, they might "hatch" sometime. But I only saw them, I did not know what they were or what they might portend. My brother and I stood spellbound before this disclosure. Eric watched the frantic circling of the ants attentively. Then he set the log back carefully, so as to crush as few of the beasts as possible, so as to restore, if possible, the protective roof over the heads of the white slugs.

There were things under things, as well as things inside things.

BUT THAT WAS another occasion. This time, I am alone with my brother who is considerably taller. He had summoned me. He had a strip of newspaper in his hand. He had a magnifying glass that he must actually have taken from our father's table. He told me to look and I saw the print on the flimsy news-sheet grown larger, but I knew the glass did this. I did not know why he had to show me this news-print. I did not read. If he wanted to show me something, it should be something more attractive, more suitable altogether. "Don't go away," he said, "it will happen in a minute." The sun was hot on our backs. The pear branch cast its late-summer shadow toward the crab-apple tree. "*Now,*" he said. Under the glass, on the paper, a dark spot appeared; almost instantaneously the newspaper burst into flames.

It was inevitable that a tall, bearded figure should appear from the Ark-like door of the outdoor study. The study was not flat on the ground but set on a series of square stone pillar-like foundations. Our father came down the steps. This picture could be found in an old collection of Bible illustrations or thumbed-over discarded reproductions of, say, the early nineteenth-century French painter, David. It is a period piece, certainly. Yet its prototype can be found engraved on Graeco-Roman medallions or outlined against the red or black background of jars or amphorae of the classic Greek period. I have said that from my reclining yet propped-up, somewhat Madame Récamier-like position on the couch, I face the wide-open double door. At the foot of the couch is the stove. Placed next the stove is the cabinet that contains the more delicate glass jars and the variously shaped bottles and Aegean vases. In the wall space, on the other side of the double door, is another case or cabinet of curiosities and antiques; on top of this case there are busts of bearded figures—Euripides? Socrates? Sophocles, certainly. There is the window now as you turn that corner, at right angles to this cabinet, and then another case that contains pottery figures and some more Greek-figure bowls. Then, the door to the waiting room. At right angles again, there is the door that leads through the laboratory-like cupboard-room or alcove, to the hall. These two last doors, the entrance door and the exit door, as I call them, are shut. The wall with the exit door is behind my head, and seated against that wall, tucked into the corner, in the three-sided niche made by the two walls and the back of the couch, is the Professor. He will sit there quietly, like an old owl in a tree. He will say nothing at all or he will lean forward and talk about something that is apparently unrelated to the progression or unfolding of our actual dream-content or thought association. He will shoot out an arm, sometimes somewhat alarmingly, to stress a point. Or he will, always making an "occasion" of it, get up and say, "Ah—now—we must celebrate *this*," and proceed to the elaborate ritual—selecting, lighting—until finally he seats himself again, while from the niche rises the smoke of burnt incense, the smouldering of his mellow, fragrant cigar.

16

LENGTH, BREADTH, thickness, the shape, the scent, the feel of things. The actuality of the present, its bearing on the past, their bearing on the future. Past, present, future, these three—but there is another time-element, popularly called the fourth-dimensional. The room has 4 sides. There are 4 seasons to a year. This 4th dimension, though it appears variously disguised and under different sub-titles, described and elaborately tabulated in the Professor's volumes—and still more elaborately detailed in the compilations of his followers, disciples and pseudo-disciples and imitators—is yet very simple. It is as simple and inevitable in the building of time-sequence as the 4th wall to a room. If we alter our course around this very room where I have been talking with the Professor, and start with the wall to my left, against which the couch is placed, and go counter-clockwise, we may number the Professor's wall with the exit door 2, the wall with the entrance door (the case of pottery images and flat Greek bowls) 3, and the wall opposite the couch 4. This wall actually is largely un-walled, as the space there is left vacant by the wide-open double doors.

The room beyond may appear very dark or there may be broken light and shadow. Or even bodily, one may walk into that room, as the Professor invited me to do one day, to look at the things on his table.

ON MY FATHER'S table there were pens and ink-bottles and a metal tray for holding the pens. He used different pens for his different inks, black and red. There was a paper-knife of Chinese or pseudo-Chinese design; a squat figure was the handle; a jar or pot on the grotesque's head held a blade that was the paper-knife, though a fret-work in low relief of leaves and tendrils gave the blade of the paper-knife an added dimension; the paper-knife was a paper-knife, at the same time it was a flat tree or pole with delicate tendrils worked over it or through it. There was an over-size pair of desk-shears, several paper-weights; one of glass showed different pictures reflected in it, if you looked into it in a certain light. It was just glass, it was a paper-weight, but it was a set of prismatic triangles, placed on another set of triangles. When you put it down, it always lay sideways; the peak, where one set of triangles met, pointed to the north pole or the south pole, or might have so pointed. There is the magnifying glass which my brother is still holding in his hand.

"BUT YOU KNOW, you children are never to play with matches." It was one of the unforgivable sins. (*Matches?*) My brother has the answer. The answer is a brave, pert rejoinder, "But we aren't playing with matches." He does not give the answer. I stand beside him. My brother is very tall. My head scarcely reaches his shoulder. I have seen the round glass in its metal frame; the straight handle is clasped by a damp, somewhat grubby paw, behind my brother's back. I do not know, he does not know that this, beside being the magnifying glass from our father's table, is a sacred symbol. It is a circle and the stem of the circle, the stalk or support of this flower, is the handle of the glass that my brother is clasping behind his back. This is the sacred *ankh*, the symbol of life in Egypt, but we do not know this—or perhaps our father does know this. He used this very sign, the circle with the supporting straight line, with an added little line, a cross, to indicate the planet Venus. I do not know if our father knows that the *ankh* is the symbol of life and that the sign he often uses at the head of one of his columns of numbers is the same sign. He writes columns and columns of numbers, yet at the top of one column he will sketch in a hieroglyph; it may stand for one of the Houses or Signs of the Zodiac, or it may be a planet simply: Jupiter or Mars or Venus. I did not know this when I stood beside my brother in the garden. I knew it a long time after but I did not understand it. It is only now as I write this that I see how my father possessed sacred symbols, how he, like the Professor, had old, old sacred objects on his study table. But the shape and form of these objects, sanctified by time, were not so identified. They were just a glass paper-weight, just a brass paper-knife or the ordinary magnifying glass that my brother is still holding in his hand.

What will my brother say? He can not say, "I brought fire from heaven." He can not answer father Zeus in elegant iambics and explain how he, Prometheus, by his wit and daring, by his love of the unknown, by his experimentation with occult, as yet unexplainable forces, has drawn down fire from the sky. It is an actual fact. But my brother has never heard of Prometheus, he doesn't know any Greek. He has taken the magnifying glass from our father's study table and that is, possibly, a sin, second only to playing with matches.

My father stamps on the flimsy charred paper. There is the smell of burnt paper and the faint trail of smoke in the still air of a late-summer day of the afternoon of the year (perhaps) 1889 or (perhaps) 1901.

I do not remember what my brother says to my father, what my father in his turn says to my brother. "You must not do it again" is implicit anyway. But the ordinary words of their common speech are sometimes above my head. I do not always even understand the words my brother uses. He is a big boy and known to be quaint and clever for his age. I am a small girl and small for my age and not very advanced. I am, in a sense, still a foreigner. There are other foreigners; they arrive from time to time, in our own house, in our grandfather's house (which is shared by an aunt and uncle), in the house across the street, in other houses, up and down Church Street. These foreigners know even less than I do of the customs of these people about us—civilized or barbaric people. Things happen that these people try to hide from us; a boy drowns in the river, a workman at the steel mill loses a limb, a foreigner or, as they say sometimes at the back door, "a little stranger" has arrived somewhat prematurely somewhere. All these mysterious, apparently unrelated events, overheard hiding under the kitchen table, or gathered or inferred, whispering with other inarticulate but none the less intuitively gifted fellow-whisperers of one's own age, and sometimes a little older, up and down Church Street, have to do with, or in some way suggest, a doctor.

19

A DOCTOR HAS a bag with strange things in it, steel and knives and scissors. Our father is not a doctor but he has a doctor's picture or a picture of doctors in his study. He is quiet and strangely tender when we are ill. He likes to tell people that he hesitated for a time before deciding on his profession, that doctors always say he should have been one of them. His voice is quiet and even and low-pitched. His voice is almost monotonously quiet. He never raises his voice. He is never irritable or angry. I never saw him really angry except two or three times in my whole life, and those were memorable occasions. Lying on this couch in the Professor's room, I feel that sometime I must recall and annotate (as it

38

were) my father's anger. But this is not one of those occasions. My father is not angry now but, though the sun is shining and the burnt paper smouldering at our feet, there is an icy chill in the air. "Perhaps," he may have said (for our father is a just man), "I did not actually *forbid* you taking the magnifying glass," for my brother has now handed it back to him. "I know that I have told you not to touch the ink-stand or take away the desk-shears or use the paste-pot for your paper soldiers. It was understood, I thought, that you did not disturb *anything* on my table."

There is frost in the air. I sidle nearer to my brother. I am implicated, though in no way blamed.

20

THERE IS an earlier occasion and again the sun is shining. From the cloth dress my mother wears, I think it must be spring, or it is an Indian-summer day, between seasons at any rate, for my mother wears a cloth dress without a coat. It is not summer, for we go into summer clothes as regularly and as inevitably as people in the tropics. We are subtropic, a town in Pennsylvania, on the map's parallel, I believe, south of Rome. Winters are cold, summers are hot, so we have the temperament of Nordics and of southerners both, harmoniously blended and altering key or vibration in strict accordance with the seasons' rules —or not, as may be. It is summer anyway in my mother's face, for she is laughing.

We have been out with her to help her with the shopping or to drop in on one of her many relatives or friends. The town contains scarcely anyone who is not a relative or friend—the "old town" at any rate; and this is the old town, for we are seated on a slight elevation of the pavement, on the curb-stone as it makes a generous curve off Church Street, under the Church and on to the stores and hotel and shopping centres of Main Street—I think it was called Main Street; it should be, anyway.

It seems odd that my mother should be laughing. My brother has defied her. He is seated firm on the curb-stone. He is not going home. As he repeats this solemnly, my mother laughs more. People stop and ask what has happened. My mother tells them and they laugh too. They stand either side of my mother, more people, friends and strangers, all laughing. "But we're collecting a crowd," she says, "we can't stay here, crowding the pavement." She obtains supporters; strangers and near-strangers repeat her words like a Greek chorus, following the promptings of their leader.

There is a slight, whispered conspiracy. The strangers melt away and my mother, with feigned indifference, strolls off. My brother knows perfectly well that she will relent, she will pretend to go away but she will wait around the corner, and if we don't follow her she will come back. He has told her that he is going away to live by himself, and he has moreover told her that his sister is coming with him. His sister waits anxiously, excited yet motionless, on the curb beside him. In addition to this final ultimatum of my brother's, we were not supposed to sit on the curb-stone. But there we sit, not "crowding the pavement" but making a little group, a design, an image at the crossroads. It appears variously in Greek tragedies with Greek names and it can be found in your original Grimm's tales or in your nursery translation, called Little-Brother, Little-Sister. One is sometimes the shadow of the other; often one is lost and the one seeks the other, as in the oldest fairy tale of the twin-brother-sister of the Nile Valley. Sometimes they are both boys like the stars Castor and Pollux, sometimes there are more than two. Actually in the case of Castor and Pollux there were four, with Helen and Clytaemnestra—the children of a Lady, we are told, and a Swan. They make a group, a constellation, they make a groove or a pattern into which or upon which other patterns fit, or are placed unfitted and are cut by circumstance to fit. In any case, it is a common-or-garden pattern though sometimes it finds its corresponding shape in heaven. And their mother has walked away. *He* knows that she will come back because he is older and is admittedly his mother's favourite. But *she* does not know this. But though her brain is in a turmoil of anxiety and pride and terror, it has not even occurred to her that she might throw her small weight into the balance of conventional behaviour by following her mother and leaving her brother to his fate.

21

THESE PICTURES are so clear. They are like transparencies, set before candles in a dark room. I may or may not have mentioned these incidents to the Professor. But they were there. Upon the elaborate build-up of past memories, across the intricate network made by the hair-lines that divided one irregular bit of the picture-puzzle from another, there fell inevitably a shadow, a writing-on-the-wall, a curve like a reversed, unfinished *S* and a dot beneath it, a question-mark, the shadow of a question— *is this it?* The question-mark threatened to shadow the apparently most satisfactory answers. No answer was final. The very answer held something of death, of finality, of Dead Sea fruit. The Professor's explanations were too illuminating, it sometimes seemed; my bat-like thought-wings would beat painfully in that sudden search-light. Or reversely, other wings (gull or skylark) that seemed about to take me right out of the lower levels of the commonplace would find themselves beating in the confined space of a wicker cage, or useless under the mesh of a bird net. But no—he did not set traps, he did not really fling nets. It was I myself, by my own subconscious volition or unconscious will, who walked or flew into them. I over-stressed or over-compensated; I purposely and painfully dwelt on certain events in the past about which I was none too happy, lest I appear to be dodging the analysis or trying to cheat the recorder of the Book of Life, to deceive the Recording Angel, in fact, in an effort to escape the Day of Judgement. Once when I painfully unravelled a dingy, carelessly woven strip of tapestry of cause and effect and related to him, in over-careful detail, some none-too-happy friendships, he waved it all aside, not bored, not grieved or surprised, but simply a little wistful, I thought, as if we had wasted precious time, our precious hours together, on something that didn't matter. "But why," he asked, "did you worry about all this? Why did you think you had to tell me? *Those two didn't count.* But you felt you wanted to tell your mother."

All this seemed almost too simple at the time. My mother was dead; things had happened before her death, ordinary as well as incredible things, that I hadn't told her. In some cases, I wanted to spare her worry and pain, as during the period of the first World War when I was in England and she was in America. Then there was her personal bereavement to consider; the death of my father followed closely on the news of the death of my older brother in France. My father, a boy of 17, and his older brother had been soldiers in our American

Civil War and my father had lost this only brother in that war; he was a mathematician, an astronomer, detached and impartial, a scholar or *savant* to use the more colourful French word. But the news of the death in action of my brother in France brought on a stroke. My father died, literally, from the shock. The Professor had had shock upon shock. But he had not died.

My father was 74 or 75 when he died—at any rate, not as old as the Professor was now. My mother had had her 70th birthday in the early 'twenties. She stayed with me for some years in London and in Vaud, Switzerland. She went back on a visit to America. I knew that she would die there; she knew it too. But I wanted to avoid thinking about this. I did not want to face this. There are various ways of trying to escape the inevitable. You can go round and round in circles like the ants under that log that Eric pried up for us. Or your psyche, your soul, can curl up and sleep like those white slugs.

22

Those two didn't count. There were two's and two's and two's in my life. There were the 2 actual brothers (the 3 of us were born within 4 years). There were the 2 half-brothers; there were the 2 tiny graves of the 2 sisters (one of those was a half-sister but there were the 2 or twin-graves). There were the 2 houses, ours and our grandparents' in the same street, with the same garden. There were the 2 Biblical towns in Pennsylvania, Bethlehem where I was born, and Philadelphia, where we moved when I was 8. There were for a time in consciousness 2 fathers and 2 mothers, for we thought that Papalie and Mamalie (our mother's parents) were our own "other" father and mother, which in fact, they were.

There were 2 of everybody (except myself) in that first house on Church Street. There were the 2 brothers who shared the same room; the 2 half-brothers might turn up at any time, together; there were the 2 maids who slept in the room over the kitchen; there were my 2 parents in their room. (There was a later addition to this Noah's Ark, but my last brother arrived after this pattern was fixed in consciousness.)

My father had married 2 times; so again, there were 2 wives, though one was dead.

Then in later life, there were 2 countries, America and England as it happened, separated by a wide gap in consciousness and a very wide stretch of sea.

The sea grows narrower, the gap in consciousness sometimes seems negligible; nevertheless there is a duality, the English-speaking peoples are related, brothers, twins even, but they are not one. So in me, 2 distinct racial or biological or psychological entities tend to grow nearer or to blend, even, as time heals old breaks in consciousness. My father's 2nd wife was the daughter of a descendant of one of the original groups of the early 18th-century, mystical Protestant order, called the Unitas Fratrum, the Bohemian or Moravian Brotherhood. Our mother's father was part mid-European by race, Polish I believe the country called itself then, when his forefathers left it, though it became German and then fluctuated like the other allied districts back and forth as in the earlier days of the Palatinate struggles. Livonia, Moravia, Bohemia—Count Zinzendorf, the founder of the renewed Bohemian brotherhood, was an Austrian, whose father was exiled or self-exiled to Upper Saxony, because of his Protestant affiliations. The Professor himself was an Austrian, a Moravian actually by birth.

23

MOTHER? Father? We have met one of them in the garden of the house on Church Street and we have seen the other further down Church Street, where the pavement makes a generous curve under the Church on to the shops. But we are not shopping. We are not calling on anyone, friend or near-friend or near or distant relative. Everyone knows our mother so we are never sure who is related and who is not— well, in a sense everyone is related for there is the Church and we all belong together in some very special way, because of our candle service on Christmas Eve which is not like what anyone else has anywhere, except in some places in Europe perhaps. Europe is far away and is a place where our parents went on their honeymoon. It is *she* who matters for she is laughing, not so much at us as with or over us and around us. *She* has bound music folios and loose sheets on the top of our piano. About *her*, there is no question. The trouble is, she knows so many people and they come and interrupt. And besides that, she likes my brother better. If I stay with my brother, become part almost of my brother, perhaps I can get nearer to *her*.

But one can never get near enough, or if one gets near, it is because one has measles or scarlet fever. *If* one could stay near her always, there would be no break in consciousness—but half a loaf is better than no bread and there are things, not altogether negligible, to be said for *him*. He has some mysterious habits, this going out at night and sleeping on the couch in his study by day. As far as that goes, there *is* his study. Provided you do not speak to him when he is sitting at his table, or disturb him when he is lying down, you are free to come and go. It is a quiet place. No one interferes or interrupts. His shelves are full of books, the room is lined with books. There is the skull on the top of the highest bookcase and the white owl under a belljar. He has more books even than our grandfather and he has that triangle paperweight that shows the things in the room repeated and in various dimensions. This, of course, I have not at the time actually put into words, hardly put into thoughts. But here I am, in some special way privileged. It is his daughter to whom he later entrusts the paper-knife; he leaves his uncut magazines and periodicals for her. She knows how to run the paper-knife carefully along under the surface of the double page, and this is especially important as her older brother is not invited to cut the pages. He has, of course, many other things to do. Our mother is a mixture of early Pennsylvania settlers, people from this island, England, and others from middle Europe—he is one thing. He is New England, though he does not live there and was not born there. He comes from those Puritan fathers who wear high peaked hats in the Thanksgiving numbers of magazines. They fought with Indians and burned witches. Their hats were like the hats the doctors wore, in the only picture that was hanging in his study. The original picture was by Rembrandt, if I am not mistaken. The half-naked man on the table was dead so it did not hurt him when the doctors sliced his arm with a knife or a pair of scissors. Is the picture called *A Lesson in Anatomy*?

It does not really matter what the picture is called. It is about doctors. There is a doctor seated at the back of the couch on which I am lying. He is a very famous doctor. He is called Sigmund Freud.

24

WE TRAVEL FAR in thought, in imagination or in the realm of memory. Events happened *as* they happened, not all of them of course but here and there a memory or a fragment of a dream-picture is actual, is real, is like a work of art or is a work of art. I have spoken of the two scenes with my brother as remaining set apart, like transparencies in a dark room, set before lighted candles. Those memories, visions, dreams, reveries—or what you will—are different. Their texture is different, the effect they have on mind and body is different. They are healing. They are real. They are as real in their dimension of length, breadth, thickness, as any of the bronze or marble or pottery or clay objects that fill the cases around the walls, that are set in elegant precision in a wide arc on the Professor's table in the other room. But we can not prove that they are real. We can discriminate as a connoisseur (as the Professor does with his priceless collection here) between the false and the true; a good copy of a rare object is not without value, but we must distinguish between a faithful copy and a spurious imitation; there are certain alloys too that may corrode and corrupt in time, and objects so blighted must be segregated or scrapped; there are priceless broken fragments that are meaningless until we find the other broken bits to match them.

There are trivial, confused dreams and there are real dreams. The trivial dream bears the same relationship to the real as a column of gutter-press news-print to a folio page of a play of Shakespeare. The dreams are as varied as are the books we read, the pictures we look at or the people we meet. "*O dreams*—we know where you Freudians think your dreams come from!" *Your young men shall see visions, and your old men shall dream dreams*. A great many of them come from the same source as the script or Scripture, the Holy Writ or Word. And there too we read of Joseph, how his brethren scoffed, *Behold this dreamer cometh*.

With the Professor, I discussed a few real dreams, some intermediate dreams that contained real imagery or whose "hieroglyph" linked with authentic images, and some quaint, trivial, mocking dreams that danced, as it were, like masquerading sweeps and May queens round the May-pole. But the most luminous, the most clearly defined of all the dream-content while I was with the Professor was the dream of the Princess, as we called her.

25

SHE WAS a dark lady. She wore a clear-coloured robe, yellow or faint-orange. It was wrapped round her as in one piece, like a sari worn as only a high-caste Indian lady could wear it. But she is not Indian, she is Egyptian. She appears at the top of a long staircase; marble steps lead down to a river. She wears no ornament, no circlet or sceptre shows her rank, but anyone would know *this is a Princess*. Down, down the steps she comes. She will not turn back, she will not stop, she will not alter the slow rhythm of her pace. She has nothing in her arms, there is no one with her; there is no extraneous object with her or about her or about the carved steps to denote any sym-bolic detail or side issue involved. There is no detail. The steps are geometrical, symmetrical and she is as abstract as a lady could be, yet she is a real entity, a real person. I, the dreamer, wait at the foot of the steps. I have no idea who I am or how I got there. There is no before or after, it is a perfect moment in time or out of time. I am concerned about something, however. I wait below the lowest step. There, in the water beside me, is a shallow basket or ark or box or boat. There is, of course, a baby nested in it. The Princess must find the baby. I know that she will find this child. I know that the baby will be protected and sheltered by her and that is all that matters.

We have all seen this picture. I pored over this picture as a child, before I could read, in our illustrated Doré Bible. But the black and white Doré illustration has nothing in common with this, except the subject. The name of this picture is *Moses in the Bulrushes* and the Professor of course knows that. The Professor and I discuss this picture. He asks if it is I, the dreamer, who am the baby in the reed basket? I don't think I am. Do I remember if the picture as I knew it as a child had any other figure? I can't remember. The Professor thinks there is the child Miriam, half concealed in the rushes; do I remember? I half remember. Am I, perhaps, the child Miriam? Or am I, after all, in my fantasy, the baby? Do I wish myself, in the deepest unconscious or subconscious layers of my being, to be the founder of a new religion?

26

ANY AMATEUR dabbler with the theories of psychoanalysis can reconstruct, even from this so-far brief evidence, the motive or material or suppressed or repressed psychic urge that projected this dream-picture. There is the little girl with her doll in her father's study. She has come to her father's study to be alone or to be alone with him. Her brother's interests are more lively and exterior and her brother does not enter readily into her doll-family games. He should be the dolls' father or the dolls' doctor, who is called in occasionally. But this does not interest him. He has soldiers and marbles and likes to race about, outdoors and indoors. Here in our father's study, we must be quiet. A girl-child, a doll, an aloof and silent father form this triangle, this family romance, this trinity which follows the recognized religious pattern: *Father,*

aloof, distant, the provider, the protector—
but a little un-get-at-able, a little too far
away and giant-like in proportion, a little
chilly withal; *Mother*, a virgin, the Virgin,
that is, an untouched child, adoring, with
faith, building a dream and the dream is
symbolized by the third member of the
trinity, the *Child*, the doll in her arms.

27

THE DOLL IS the dream or the symbol of the
dream of this particular child, as these various Ra, Nut, Hathor, Isis, and Ka figures
that are dimly apprehended on their shelves
or on the Professor's table in the other
room are the dream or the symbol of the
dream of other aspiring and adoring souls.
The childhood of the individual is the
childhood of the race, we have noted, the
Professor has written somewhere. The
child in me has gone. The child has vanished and yet it is not dead. This contact
with the Professor intensifies or projects
this dream of a Princess, the river, the
steps, the child. The river is an Egyptian
river, the Nile; the Princess is an Egyptian
lady. Egypt is present, as I say, actually or

by inference or suggestion, in the old-fashioned print or engraving of the Temple at Karnak, hanging on the wall above me, as well as in the dimly outlined egg-shaped Ra or Nut or Ka figures on the Professor's desk in the other room. A Queen or Princess is obvious mother-symbol; moreover, there had been casual references, from time to time, to the Professor's French translator, Madame Marie Bonaparte, "the Princess" or "our Princess," as the Professor calls her.

Perhaps here too, as on the occasion of the Professor's birthday in the house at Döbling, I wanted something different or I wanted to give the Professor something different. Princess George of Greece had been consistently helpful and used her influence in the general interests of the Psycho-Analytical Association. She was "our Princess" in that; as Marie Bonaparte, she had translated the Professor's difficult German into French and was ready to stand by him now that the Nazi peril was already threatening Vienna. She was "our Princess" in the world, devoted and influential. But is it possible that I sensed another world, another Princess? Is it possible that I (leaping over every sort of intellectual impediment and obstacle) not wished

only, but *knew*, the Professor would be
born again?

28

FOR THINGS had happened in my life, pictures, "real dreams," actual psychic or occult experiences that were superficially, at
least, outside the province of established
psychoanalysis. But I am working with the
old Professor himself; I want his opinion
on a series of events. It is true, I had not
discussed these experiences openly, but I
had sought help from one or two (to my
mind) extremely wise and gifted people in
the past and they had not helped me. At
least, they had not been able to lay, as it
were, the ghost. If the Professor could not
do this, I thought, nobody could. I could
not get rid of the experience by writing
about it. I had tried that. There was no use
telling the story, into the air, as it were, re-
peatedly, like the Ancient Mariner who
plucked at the garments of the wedding
guest with that skinny hand. My own
skinny hand would lay, as it were, the
cards on the table—here and now—here
with the old Professor. He was more than

the world thought him—that I well knew. If he could not "tell my fortune," nobody else could. He would not call it telling fortunes—heaven forbid! But we would lead up to the occult phenomena, we would show him how it happened. That, at least, we could do—in part, at any rate. I could say, I did say that I had had a number of severe shocks; the news of the death of my father, following the death in action of my brother in France, came to me when I was alone outside London in the early spring of that bad influenza winter of 1919. I myself was waiting for my second child—I had lost the first in 1915, from shock and repercussions of war news broken to me in a rather brutal fashion.

The second child, for some reason, I knew, must be born. Oh, she would be born, all right, though it was an admitted scientific fact that a waiting mother, stricken with that pneumonia, double pneumonia, would not live. She might live—yes —but then the child would not. They rarely both live, if ever! But there were reasons for us both living, so we did live. At some cost, however! The material and spiritual burden of pulling us out of danger fell upon a young woman whom I had only recently met—anyone who knows me knows who this person is. Her pseudonym is Bryher and we all call her Bryher. If I got well, she would herself see that the baby was protected and cherished and she would take me to a new world, a new life, to the land, spiritually of my predilection, geographically of my dreams. We would go to Greece, it could be arranged. It was arranged, though we two were the first unofficial visitors to Athens after that war. This was spring, 1920. This spring of 1920 held for me many unresolved terrors, perils, heart-aches, dangers, physical as well as spiritual or intellectual. If I had been a little maladjusted or even mildly deranged, it would have been no small wonder. But of a series of strange experiences, the Professor picked out only one as being dangerous, or hinting of danger or a dangerous tendency or symptom. I do not yet quite see why he picked on the writing-on-the-wall as the danger-signal, and omitted what to my mind were tendencies or events that were equally important or equally "dangerous." However, as the Professor picked on the writing-on-the-wall as the most dangerous or the only actually dangerous "symptom," we will review it here.

29

THE SERIES of shadow- or of light-pictures I saw projected on the wall of a hotel bed-room in the Ionian island of Corfu, at the end of April, 1920, belong in the sense of quality and intensity, of clarity and authenticity, to the same psychic category as the dream of the Princess, the Pharaoh's daughter, coming down the stairs. For myself I consider this sort of dream or projected picture or vision as a sort of half-way state between ordinary dream and the vision of those who, for lack of a more definite term, we must call psychics or clairvoyants. Memories too, like the two I have recorded of my father in the garden and my mother on Church Street, are in a sense super-memories; they are ordinary, "normal" memories but retained with so vivid a detail that they become almost events out of time, like the Princess dream and the writing-on-the-wall. They are steps in the so-far superficially catalogued or built-up mechanism of supernormal, abnormal (or subnormal) states of mind. Steps? The Princess is coming down the steps from a house or palace or hall, far beyond our human habitation. The steps lead down to a river, the river of life presumably, that river named Nile in Egypt. She is "our Princess"—that is, she is specifically the Professor's Princess and mine, "our" personal guardian or inspiration. She is peculiarly "his" Princess for this is a life-wish, apparently, that I have projected into or unto an image of the Professor's racial, ancestral background. We have talked of his age; his 77 symbolized occult power and mystery to me. I frankly told him this without fear of being snubbed or thought ridiculous or superstitious. It is important to me, that 77, and I have a 7 or will acquire one a few months after his May birthday. Mine is, at the time, a 47, so there is 30 years difference in our ages. But ages? Around us are the old images or "dolls" of pre-dynastic Egypt, and Moses was perhaps not yet born when that little Ra or Nut or Ka figure on the Professor's desk was first hammered by a forger-priest of Ptah on the banks of the Nile.

30

I AM NO DOUBT impressed, probably not a little envious of that gifted lady, "our Princess" as the Professor calls her. I, no doubt, unconsciously covet her worldly position, her intellectual endowments, her power of translating the difficult, scholarly, beautiful German of Sigmund Freud into no doubt equally distinguished and beautiful French. I can not compete with her. Consciously, I do not feel any desire to do so. But unconsciously, I probably wish to be another equal factor or have equal power of benefiting and protecting the Professor. I am also concerned, though I do not openly admit this, about the Professor's attitude to a future life. One day, I was deeply distressed when the Professor spoke to me about his grandchildren—what would become of them? He asked me that, as if the future of his immediate family were the only future to be considered. There was, of course, the perfectly secured future of his own work, his books. But there was a more imminent, a more immediate future to consider. It worried me to feel that he had no idea—it seemed impossible—really no idea that he would "wake up" when he shed the frail locust-husk of his years, and find himself alive.

31

I DID NOT say this to him. I did not really realize how deeply it concerned me. It was a *fact*, but a fact that I had not personally or concretely resolved. I had accepted as part of my racial, my religious inheritance, the abstract idea of immortality, of the personal soul's existence in some form or other, after it has shed the outworn or outgrown body. The *Chambered Nautilus* of the New England poet, Oliver Wendell Holmes, had been a great favourite of mine as a school-girl; I did not think of the poem then, but its metres echo in my head now as I write this. *Till thou at length art free*, the last stanza ends, *Leaving thine outgrown shell by life's unresting sea!* And *Build thee more stately mansions, O my soul* is another line, and with the Professor, I did feel that I had reached the high-water mark of achievement; I mean, I felt that to meet him at 47, and to be accepted by him as analysand or student, seemed to crown all my other personal contacts and relationships, justify all the spiral-like meanderings of my mind and body. I had come home, in fact. And another poem comes inevitably to prompt me:

On desperate seas long wont to roam,
  Thy hyacinth hair, thy classic face,
Thy Naiad airs, have brought me home
  To the glory that was Greece
  And the grandeur that was Rome.

This is, of course, Edgar Allan Poe's much-quoted *Helen*, and my mother's name was Helen.

32

THE PROFESSOR translated the pictures on the wall, or the picture-writing on the wall of a hotel bedroom in Corfu, the Greek Ionian island, that I saw projected there in the spring of 1920, as a desire for union with my mother. I was physically in Greece, in Hellas (Helen). I had come home to the glory that was Greece. Perhaps my trip to Greece, that spring, might have been interpreted as a flight from reality. Perhaps my experiences there might be translated as another flight—from a flight. There were wings anyway. I may say that never before and never since have I had an experience of this kind. I saw a dim shape forming on the wall between the foot of the bed and the wash-stand. It was late afternoon; the wall was a dull, mat ochre. I thought, at first, it was sunlight flickering from the shadows cast from or across the orange trees in full leaf and fruit and flower outside the bedroom window. But I realized instantly that our side of the house was already in early shadow. The pictures on the wall were like colourless transfers or 'calcomanias, as we pretentiously called them as children. The first was head and shoulders, three-quarter face, no marked features, a stencil or stamp of a soldier or airman, but the figure was dim light on shadow, not shadow on light. It was a silhouette cut of light, not shadow, and so impersonal it might have been anyone, of almost any country. And yet there was a distinctly familiar line about that head with the visored cap; immediately it was *somebody*, unidentified indeed, yet suggesting a question—dead brother? lost friend?

Then there was the conventional outline of a goblet or cup, actually suggesting the mystic chalice, but it was the familiar goblet shape we all know, with round base and glass-stem. This chalice is as large as the head of the soldier, or rather it simply takes up the same amount of space, as if they were both formal patterns stamped on picture-cards, or even (now that I think of it) on playing cards. I have said, with the Professor, that I would lay my cards on the table. These were those cards; so far, two of them. The third follows at once or I now perceive it. It is a simple design in perspective, at least suggesting perspective after the other two flat patterns. It is a circle or two circles, the base the larger of the two; it is joined by three lines, not flat as I say but in perspective, a simple object to draw, once the idea of tilting the planes to give the idea of space is understood. And this object is so simple yet so homely that I think again, "It's a shadow thrown." Actually, it could not have been, as this shadow was "light"; but the exact replica of this pattern was set on the upper shelf of the old-fashioned wash-stand, along with toothbrush mug, soap-dish and those various oddments. It was exactly the stand for the small spirit-lamp we had with us. (*Spirit-lamp?*) And I know that, if these objects are projected outward from my own brain, this is a neat trick, a short-cut, a pun, a sort of joke. For the three-legged lamp-stand in the miscellaneous clutter on the wash-stand is none other than our old friend, the tripod of classic Delphi. So the tripod, this venerated object of the cult of the sun god, symbol of poetry and prophecy, is linked by association with this most ordinary little metal frame that fits into the small saucepan and is used as a support for it when we boil water for that extra sustaining cup of tea upstairs in our room. The tripod then is linked in thought with something friendly and ordinary, the third or second member of my travellers' set, used as base for the flat spirit-lamp and support for the aluminum container. The tripod now becomes all the more an object to be venerated. At any rate, there it is, the third of my cards on the table.

33

SO FAR, SO GOOD—or so far, so dangerous, so abnormal a "symptom." The writing, at least, is consistent. It is composed by the same person, it is drawn or written by the same hand. Whether that hand or person is myself, projecting the images as a sign, a warning or a guiding sign-post from my own subconscious mind, or whether they are projected from outside—they are at least clear enough, abstract and yet at the same time related to images of our ordinary time and space. But here I pause or the hand pauses—it is as if there were a slight question as to the conclusion or direction of the symbols. I mean, it was as if a painter had stepped back from a canvas the better to regard the composition of the picture, or a musician had paused at the music-stand, perhaps for a moment, in doubt as to whether he would continue his theme, or wondering perhaps in a more practical manner if he could himself turn the page on the stand before him without interrupting the flow of the music. That is in myself too—a wonder as to the seemliness, or the safety even, of continuing this experience or this experiment. For my head, although it can not have taken very long in clock-time for these pictures to form there, is already warning me that this is an unusual dimension, an unusual way to *think*, that my brain or mind may not be equal to the occasion. Perhaps in that sense the Professor was right (actually, he was always right, though we sometimes translated our thoughts into different languages or mediums). But there I am seated on the old-fashioned Victorian sofa in the Greek island hotel bedroom, and here I am reclining on the couch in the Professor's room, telling him this, and here again am I, 10 years later, seated at my desk in my own room in London. But there is no clock-time, though we are fastidiously concerned with time and with a formal handling of a subject which has no racial and no time-barriers. Here is this hieroglyph of the unconscious or subconscious of the Professor's discovery and life-study, the hieroglyph actually in operation before our very eyes. But it is no easy matter to sustain this mood, this "symptom" or this inspiration.

And there I sat and there is my friend Bryher who has brought me to Greece. I can turn now to her, though I do not budge an inch or break the sustained crystal-gazing stare at the wall before me. I say to Bryher, "There have been pictures here —I thought they were shadows at first, but they are light, not shadow. They are quite simple objects—but of course it's very strange. I can break away from them now, if I want—it's just a matter of concentrating—what do you think? Shall I stop? Shall I go on?" Bryher says without hesitation, "Go on."

34

WHILE I WAS speaking to Bryher, there is a sort of pictorial buzzing—I mean, about the base of the tripod, there are small creatures, but these are in black; they move about, in and around the base of the tripod, but they are very small; they are like ants swarming, or very small half-winged insects that have not yet learnt to fly. Fly? They are flies, it seems—but no, they are tiny people, all in black or outlined as in, or with, shadow, in distinction to the figures of the three "cards" already described. They are not a symbol of themselves, they are simply a sort of dust, a cloud or a swarm of small midges that move back and forth, but on one level, as if walking rather than flying. Even as I consider this new aspect of the writing, I am bothered, annoyed—just as one is when suddenly in a country lane one is beset in the evening light by a sudden swarm of midges. They are not important but it would be a calamity if one of them got stuck in one's eye. There was that sort of feeling; people, people—did they annoy me so? Would they perhaps eventually cloud my vision or, worse still, would one of them get "stuck in my eye"? They were people, they were annoying—I did not hate people, I did not especially resent any one person. I had known such extraordinarily gifted and charming people. They had made much of me or they had slighted me and yet neither praise nor neglect mattered in the face of the gravest issues—life, death. (I had had my child, I was alive.) And yet, so oddly, I knew that this experience, this writing-on-the-wall before me, could not be shared with them—could not be shared with anyone except the girl who stood so bravely there beside me. This girl had said without hesitation, "Go on." It was she really who had the detachment and the integrity of the Pythoness of Delphi. But it was I, battered and disassociated from my American family and my English friends, who was seeing the pictures, who was reading the writing or who was granted the inner vision. Or perhaps in some sense, we were "seeing" it together, for without her, admittedly, I could not have gone on.

35

YET, ALTHOUGH now assured of her support, my own head is splitting with the ache of concentration. I know that if I let go, lessen the intensity of my stare and shut my eyes or even blink my eyes, to rest them, the pictures will fade out. My curiosity is insatiable. This has never happened to me before, it may never happen again. I am not actually analysing this as I watch the pictures, but it seems now possible that the mechanism of their projection (from within or from without) had something to do with, or in some way was related to, my feelings for the shrine at Delphi. Actually, we had intended stopping off at Itea; we had come from Athens, by boat through the Corinthian canal and up the Gulf of Corinth. Delphi and the shrine of Helios (Hellas, Helen) had been really the main objective of my journey. Athens came a very close second in affection; however, having left Athens, we were informed when the boat stopped at Itea that it was absolutely impossible for two ladies alone, at that time, to make the then dangerous trip on the winding road to Delphi, that in imagination I saw so clearly tucked away under Parnassus. Bryher and I were forced to content ourselves with a somewhat longer stay than was first planned in the beautiful island of Corfu.

But the idea of Delphi had always touched me very deeply and Bryher and I, back in that winter London of the previous spring—it was a winter London that spring —had talked of the famous sacred way. She herself had visited these places with her father before the 1914 war and I had once said to her, while convalescing from the 1919 illness, "If I could only feel that I could walk the sacred way to Delphi, I know I would get well." But no, now that we were so near, we could not go to Delphi. We were going in another direction, Brindisi, Rome, Paris, London. Already our half-packed bags, typewriter, books lay strewn about; we obviously *were* leaving. And we were not leaving Corfu in order to return to Athens, as we had talked of doing when we first landed at Corfu, with the thought of a possible arrangement, after all, with a party from one of the archaeological schools at Athens, from Athens itself, overland to Delphi. Travel was difficult, the country itself in a state of political upheaval; chance hotel acquaintances expressed surprise that two women alone had been allowed to come at all at that time. We were always "two women alone" or "two ladies alone," but we were not alone.

36

THERE HAD BEEN writing-on-walls before, in Biblical, in classic literature. At least, all through time, there had been a tradition of warnings or messages from another world or another state of being. Delphi, specifically, was the shrine of the Prophet and Musician, the inspiration of artists and the patron of physicians. Was not the "blameless physician," Asklepios himself, reputed to be Phoebus Apollo's own son? Religion, art and medicine, through the latter ages, became separated; they grow further apart from day to day. These three working together, to form a new vehicle of expression or a new form of thinking or of living, might be symbolized by the tripod, the third of the images on the wall before me, the third of the "cards" I threw down, as it were on the table, for the benefit of the old Professor. The tripod, we know, was the symbol of prophecy, prophetic utterance or occult or hidden knowledge; the Priestess or Pythoness of Delphi sat on the tripod while she pronounced her verse couplets, the famous Delphic utterances which it was said could be read two ways.

We can read my writing, the fact that there was writing, in two ways or in more than two ways. We can read or translate it as a suppressed desire for forbidden "signs and wonders," breaking bounds, a suppressed desire to be a Prophetess, to be important anyway, megalomania they call it— a hidden desire to "found a new religion" which the Professor ferreted out in the later Moses picture. Or this writing-on-the-wall is merely an extension of the artist's mind, a *picture* or an illustrated poem, taken out of the actual dream or day-dream content and projected from within (though apparently from outside), really a high-powered *idea*, simply over-stressed, *over-thought*, you might say, an echo of an idea, a reflection of a reflection, a "freak" thought that had got out of hand, gone too far, a "dangerous symptom."

37

BUT SYMPTOM or inspiration, the writing continues to write itself or be written. It is admittedly picture-writing, though its symbols can be translated into terms of to-day; it is Greek in spirit, rather than Egyptian. The original or basic image, however, is common to the whole race and applicable to almost any time.

38

SO FAR THE PICTURES, the transfers or " 'calcomanias," have run level on the wall space between the foot of the bed and the washstand. Now they take an upward course or seem about to do so. The "buzzing" seems to have ceased or the black flies have flown away or the shadow-people faded out. The first three pictures or "cards on the table" were static, they were there complete; or dimly there, they became less dim as the outline and the meaning became recognizable. But this picture or symbol begins to draw itself before my eyes. *The moving finger writes*. Two dots of light are placed or appear on the space above the rail of the wash-stand, and a line forms, but so very slowly—as if the two rather heavy dots elongated from their own centres, as if they faded in intensity as two lines emerged, slowly moving toward one another. They will meet, it is evident, and from the pattern (two dots on a blackboard) we will get a single line. I do not know how long it took for these two frail lines to meet and then to remain one, intensified or in italics, underlined as it were. One line? It may have taken a split fraction of a second to form, but now I am perfectly well aware that this concentration is a difficult matter. My facial muscles seem stiff with the effort and I may become frozen like one of those enemies of Athené, the goddess of wisdom, to whom Perseus showed the Gorgon head. Am I looking at the Gorgon head, a suspect, an enemy to be dealt with? Or am I myself Perseus, the hero who is fighting for Truth and Wisdom? But Perseus could find his way about with winged sandals and the cloak of invisibility. Moreover, he himself could wield the ugly weapon of the Gorgon's severed head, because Athené (or was it Hermes, Mercury?) had told him what to do. He was himself to manipulate his weapon, this ugly severed head of the enemy of Wisdom and Beauty, by looking at it in the polished metal of his shield. Even he, the half-god or hero, would be turned to stone, frozen if he regarded too closely and without the shield to protect him, in its new quality of looking-glass or reflector, the ugly Head or Source of evil. So I, though I did not make this parallel at the time, still wondered. But even as I wondered, I kept the steady concentrated gaze at the wall before me.

39

THERE IS ONE LINE clearly drawn, but before I have actually recovered from this, or have had time to take breath, as it were, another two dots appear and I know that another line will form in the same way. So it does, each line is a little shorter than its predecessor, so at last, there it is, this series of foreshortened lines that make a ladder or give the impression of a ladder set up there on the wall above the wash-stand. It is a ladder of light, but even now I may not take time, as I say, to draw breath. I may be breathing naturally but I have the feeling of holding my breath under water. As if I were searching under water for some priceless treasure, and if I bobbed up to the surface the clue to its whereabouts would be lost for ever. So I, though seated upright, am in a sense diving, head-down under water—in another element, and as I seem now so near to getting the answer or finding the treasure, I feel that my whole life, my whole being, will be blighted for

ever if I miss this chance. I must not lose
grip, I must not lose the end of the picture
and so miss the meaning of the whole, so
far painfully perceived. I must hold on
here or the picture will blur over and the
sequence be lost. In a sense, it seems I am
drowning; already half-drowned to the
ordinary dimensions of space and time, I
know that I must drown, as it were, completely in order to come out on the other
side of things (like Alice with her looking-
glass or Perseus with his mirror). I must
drown completely and come out on the
other side, or rise to the surface after the
third time down, not dead to this life but
with a new set of values, my treasure
dredged from the depth. I must be born
again or break utterly.

40

THESE LINES SEEM to take such a long time
to form separately. Perhaps they are symbolic ages or aeons. Anyhow, I have been
able to concentrate, to hold the picture so
far. There are maybe 7 rungs to this ladder, maybe 5; I did not count them. They
are symbolic anyway, the ladder itself is a

symbol well authenticated; it is Jacob's ladder if you will; it is a symbol common to all religious myth or lore.

But fortunately the last figure to form does so, quickly; at least, there seems less strain and worry of waiting now. There she is, I call her she; I call her Niké, Victory. She is facing the wall or moving as against the wall up from the last rung of the ladder and she moves or floats swiftly enough. To my right, to her right on the space between the ladder and the mirror-frame above the wash-stand, there is a series of broken curves. Actually, they are above the ladder, not touching the angel who brushes past them. I realize that this decorative detail is in a sense suggested by the scrollwork of the mirror-frame, but as in the case of the tripod (also suggested by, or reminding me of a natural homely object on the stand there), it can not be a replica of it, a shadow of it, for again the scrollwork is drawn in *light* and would not anyway match a shadow direction even if shadow could be thrown. The S or half-S faces the angel; that is, the series of the S-pattern opens out in the direction of the angel; they are like question-marks without the dot beneath them. I did not know what this scrollwork indicated; I thought at the time that it was a mere wave-like decorative detail. But now I think this inverted *S*-pattern may have represented a series of question-marks, the questions that have been asked through the ages, that the ages will go on asking.

41

VICTORY, NIKÉ, as I called her exactly then and there, goes on. She is a common-or-garden angel, like any angel you may find on an Easter or Christmas card. Her back is toward me, she is simply outlined but very clearly outlined like the first three symbols or "cards." But unlike them, she is not flat or static, she is in space, in unwalled space, not flat against the wall, though she moves upward as against its surface. She is a moving-picture, and fortunately she moves swiftly. Not swiftly exactly but with a sure floating that at least gives my mind some rest, as if my mind had now escaped the bars of that ladder, no longer climbing or caged but free and with wings. On she goes. Above her head, to her left in the space left vacant on this black-board (or light-board) or screen, a series of tent-like triangles forms. I say tent-like triangles, for though they are simple triangles they suggest tents to me. I feel that the Niké is about to move into and through the tents, and this she exactly does. So far—so good. But this is enough. I drop my head in my hands; it is aching with this effort of concentration, but I feel that I have seen the picture. I thought, "Niké, Victory," and even as I thought it, it seemed to me that this Victory was not now, it was another Victory; in which case there would be another war. When that war had completed itself, rung by rung or year by year, I, personally (I felt), would be free, I myself would go on in another, a winged dimension. For the tents, it seemed to me, were not so much the symbolic tents of the past battle-fields, the near past or the far past, but tents or shelters to be set up in another future contest. The picture now seemed to be something to do with another war, but even at that there would be Victory. Niké, Victory seemed to be the clue, seemed to be my own especial sign or part of my hieroglyph. We had visited in Athens, only a short time ago, the tiny Temple of Victory that stands on the rock of the Acropolis, to your right as you turn off from the Propylaea. I must hold on to this one word. I thought, "Niké,

Victory." I thought, "Helios, the sun . . ."
And I shut off, "cut out" before the final
picture, before (you might say) the ex-
plosion took place.

But though I admit to myself that now I
have had enough, maybe just a little too
much, Bryher, who has been waiting by
me, carries on the "reading" where I left
off. Afterwards she told me that she had
seen nothing on the wall there, until I
dropped my head in my hands. She had
been there with me, patient, wondering, no
doubt deeply concerned and not a little
anxious as to the outcome of my state or
mood. But as I relaxed, let go, from complete physical and mental exhaustion, she
saw what I did not see. It was the last section of the series, or the last concluding
symbol—perhaps that "determinative" that
is used in the actual hieroglyph, the picture
that contains the whole series of pictures in
itself or helps clarify or explain them. In
any case, it is apparently a clear enough picture or symbol. She said, it was a circle like
the sun-disc and a figure within the disc; a
man, she thought, was reaching out to draw
the image of a woman (my Niké?) into
the sun beside him.

42

THE YEARS BETWEEN seemed a period of waiting, of marking time. There was a growing feeling of stagnation, of lethargy, clearly evident among many of my own contemporaries. Those who were aware of the trend of political events, on the other hand, were almost too clever, too politically minded, too high-powered intellectually for me altogether. What I seemed to sense and wait for was frowned upon by the first group, though I learned very early not to air my thoughts and fears; they were morbid, they were too self-centered and introspective altogether. Why—my brother-in-law spent such a happy holiday in the Black Forest (with—so-and-so— chapter and verse) and the food was so good—everybody was so hospitable and so very charming. If, on the other hand, I ventured a feeble opinion to the second group, I was given not chapter and verse so much as the whole outpouring of predigested voluminous theories. My brain staggers now when I remember the deluge of brilliant talk I was inflicted with; what would happen if, and who would come to power when—but with all their abstract clear-sightedness, this second group seemed as muddled, as lethargic in their own way, as the first. At least, their theories and their accumulated data seemed unrooted, raw. But this, I admit—yes, I know—was partly due to my own hopeless feeling in the face of brilliant statisticians and one-track-minded theories. *Where is this taking you,* I wanted to shout at both parties. One refused to admit the fact that the flood was coming—the other counted the nails and measured the planks with endless exact mathematical formulas, but didn't seem to have the very least idea of how to put the Ark together.

43

ALREADY IN VIENNA, the shadows were lengthening or the tide was rising. The signs of grim coming events, however, manifested in a curious fashion. There were, for instance, occasional coquettish, confetti-like showers from the air, gilded paper swastikas and narrow strips of printed paper like the ones we pulled out of our Christmas bon-bons, those gay favours that we called "caps" as children in America and that English children call "crackers."

The party had begun, or this was preliminary to the birthday or the wedding. I
stooped to scrape up a handful of these confetti-like tokens as I was leaving the Hotel
Regina one morning. They were printed
on those familiar little oblongs of thin
paper that fell out of the paper cap when it
was unfolded at the party; we called them
mottoes. These mottoes were short and
bright and to the point. One read in clear
primer-book German, "Hitler gives bread,"
"Hitler gives work," and so on. I wondered
if I should enclose this handful in a letter
to one of my first group of friends in London—or to one of the second. I had a mis-
chievous picture of this gay shower falling
on a carpet in Kensington or Knights-
bridge or on a bare floor in a Chelsea or
Bloomsbury studio. It would be a good
joke. The paper was crisp and clean, the
gold clear as Danaë's legendary shower, and
the whole savoured of birthday cake and
candles or fresh-bought Christmas-tree
decorations. The gold, however, would not
stay bright nor the paper crisp very long,
for people passed to and fro across Freiheitsplatz and along the pavement, tram-
pling over this Danaë shower, not taking
any notice. Was I the only person in Vienna who had stooped to scrape up a hand-

ful of these tokens? It seemed so. One of the hotel porters emerged with a long-handled brush-broom. As I saw him begin methodically sweeping the papers off the pavement, I dropped my handful in the gutter.

44

THERE WERE OTHER swastikas. They were chalk ones now; I followed them down Berggasse as if they had been chalked on the pavement especially for my benefit. They led to the Professor's door—maybe, they passed on down another street to another door but I did not look any further. No one brushed these swastikas out. It is not so easy to scrub death-head chalk-marks from a pavement. It is not so easy and it is more conspicuous than sweeping tinsel paper into a gutter. And this was a little later.

45

THEN THERE WERE rifles. They were
stacked neatly. They stood in bivouac for-
mations at the street corners. It must have
been a week-end; I don't remember. I could
verify the actual date of their appearance
by referring to my note-books, but it is
the general impression that concerns us,
rather than the historical or political sequence. They were not German guns—but
perhaps they were; anyway, these were
Austrian soldiers. The stacks of rifles gave
the streets a neat, finished effect, as of an
1860 print. They seemed old-fashioned, the
soldiers seemed old-fashioned; I was no
doubt reminded of familiar pictures of our
American Civil War. This was some sort
of civil war. No one would explain it to
me. The hall porter, usually so talkative,
was embarrassed when I questioned him.
Well, I must not involve him in any discussion or dangerous statement of opinion.
I went out anyway. There were some people about and the soldiers were out of a
picture or a film of a reconstructed Civil
War period. They did not seem very
formidable. I had meant to go to the opera—
it was late afternoon or early evening—so I
might as well go to the opera, if there were

an opera, as mope in my room or loiter about the hotel, wondering and watching. When challenged on one of the main thoroughfares, I said simply, in my sketchy German, that I was a visitor in Vienna; they called me the English lady at the hotel, so I said I was from England, which in fact I was. What was I doing? Where was I going? I said I was going to the opera, if I was not disturbing them or getting in their way. There was a little whispering and shuffling and I was embarrassed to find that I had attracted the attention of the officers and had almost a guard of honour to the steps of the opera house, where there were more guns and soldiers, seated on the steps and standing at attention on the pavement. It seemed that nothing, at any rate, could stop the opera. I stayed for part of the performance of—I don't remember what it was—and had no trouble finding my way back.

46

THEN IT WAS QUIET and the hotel lobby seemed strangely empty. Even the hall porter disappeared from behind his desk.

Maybe, this was the following Monday; in any case, I was due at Berggasse for my usual session. The little maid, Paula, peered through a crack in the door, hesitated, then furtively ushered me in. She did not wear her pretty cap and apron. Evidently, she was not expecting me. "But—but no one has come to-day; no one has gone out." All right, would she explain to the Professor, in case he did not want to see me. She opened the waiting-room door. I waited as usual in the room, with the round table, the odds and ends of old papers and magazines. There were the usual framed photographs; among them, Dr. Havelock Ellis and Dr. Hanns Sachs greeted me from the wall. There was the honorary diploma that had been presented to the Professor in his early days by the small New England university. There was also a bizarre print or engraving of some nightmare horror, a "Buried Alive" or some such thing, done in Düreresque symbolic detail. There were long lace curtains at the window, like a "room in Vienna" in a play or film.

The Professor opened the inner door after a short interval. Then I sat on the couch. The Professor said, "But why did you come? No one has come here to-day,

no one. What is it like outside? Why did
you come out?"

I said, "It's very quiet. There doesn't
seem to be anyone about in the streets. The
hotel seems quiet, too. But otherwise, it's
much the same as usual." He said, "Why
did you come?" It seemed to puzzle him, he
did not seem to understand what had
brought me.

47

WHAT DID HE expect me to say? I don't
think I said it. My being there surely expressed it? *I am here because no one else
has come.* As if again, symbolically, I must
be different. Where was the Flying Dutchman? Or the American lady-doctor whom
I had not seen? There were only four of
us at that time, I believe, rather special people. It is true that Mrs. Burlingham, Miss
Anna Freud's devoted friend, and the Professor's disciple or pupil, had an apartment, further up the stairs. I had gone up
there to tea one day before my session here.
The Professor was not really alone. The
envoys of the Princess, too, I had been informed, were waiting on the door-steps of

various legations and they would inform her of any actual threat to the Professor's personal safety. But, in a sense, I was the only one who had come from the outside; little Paula substantiated that when she peered so fearfully through the crack in the front door. Again, I was different. I had made a unique gesture, although actually I felt my coming was the merest courtesy; this was our usual time of meeting, our session, our "hour" together. I did not know what the Professor was thinking. He could not be thinking, "I am an old man—*you do not think it worth your while to love me.*" Or if he remembered having said that, this surely was the answer to it.

48

IT MAY HAVE BEEN that day or another that the Professor spoke of his grandchildren. In any case, whenever it was, I felt a sudden gap, a severance, a chasm or a schism in consciousness, which I tried to conceal from him. It was so tribal, so conventionally Mosaic. As he ran over their names and the names of their parents, one felt the old impatience, a sort of intellectual eye-strain, the old boredom of looking out historical, genealogical references in a small-print school or Sunday-school Bible. It was Genesis but not the very beginning. Not the exciting verses about the birds and the reptiles, the trees, the sun and the moon, those greater and lesser lights. He was worried about them (and no small wonder), but I was worried about something else. I did not then realize the reason for my anxiety. I knew the Professor would move on somewhere else, before so very long, but it seemed the eternal life he visualized was in the old Judaic tradition. He would live for ever like Abraham, Isaac and Jacob, in his children's children, multiplied like the sands of the sea. That is how it seemed to me his mind was working, and that is how, faced with the blank wall of danger, of physical annihilation, his mind would work.

At least, there was that question between us, "What will become of my grandchildren?" He was looking ahead but his concern for immortality was translated into terms of grandchildren. He would live in them; he would live in his books, of course; I may have murmured something vaguely to the effect that future generations would continue to be grateful to his written word; that, I may have mentioned—I am sure I did

sometime or other, on that or another occasion. But though a sincere tribute, those
words were, or would be, in a sense, superficial. They would fall flat, somehow. It
was so very obvious that his work would
live beyond him. To express this adequately
would be to delve too deep, to become involved in technicalities, and at the same
time it would be translating my admiration for what he stood for, what actually he
was, into terms a little too formal, too prim
and precise, too conventional, too banal,
too *polite*.

I did not want to murmur conventional
words; plenty of people had done that. If I
could not say exactly what I wanted to say,
I would not say anything, just as on his
77th birthday, if I could not find what I
wanted to give, I would not give anything.
I did find what I wanted, that cluster of
gardenias, somewhat later; that offering
was in the autumn of 1938. And these
words, the words that I could not speak
then, too, come somewhat later, in the
autumn of 1944. The flowers and the
words bear this in common, they are what
I want, what I waited to find for the Professor, "to greet the return of the Gods."
It is true, "other people read: Goods." A
great many people had read "goods" and

would continue to do so. But the Professor knew, he must have known, that, by implication, he himself was included in the number of those Gods. He himself already counted as immortal.

49

I DID NOT know exactly *who* he was and yet it seems very obvious now. Long ago, in America, I had a peculiar dream or merely a flash of vision. I was not given to these things, though as a small child, in common with many other small children, I had had one or two visionary or supernormal experiences. This time I must have been 18 or 19. The picture or segment of picture impressed me so much that I tried to identify it. It was not a very sensational experience. The vision or picture was simply this: before sleeping or just on wakening, there was a solid shape before my eyes, no luminous cloud-pictures or vague fantasy, but an altar-shaped block of stone; this was divided into two sections by the rough stone marking; it was hardly a carved line but it was definitely a division of the surface of the rough stone into two halves.

In one half or section, there was a serpent, roughly carved; he was conventionally coiled with head erect; on the other side, there was a roughly incised, naturalistic yet conventionally drawn thistle. Why this?

It is odd to think, at this very late date, that it was Ezra Pound who helped me interpret this picture. Ezra was a year older; I had known him since I was 15. I do not think I spoke of this to anyone but Ezra and a girl, Frances Josepha, with whom later I took my first trip to Europe. Ezra at that time was staying with his parents in a house outside Philadelphia, for the summer months. It was there, one afternoon, that Ezra said, "I have an idea about your snake on a brick," as he called it. We went into the study or library—it was a furnished house, taken over from friends—and Ezra began jerking out various reference books and concordances. He seemed satisfied in the end that this was a flash-back in time or a prevision of some future event that had to do with Aesculapius or Asklepios, the human or half-human, half-divine child of Phoebus Apollo, who was slain by the thunder-bolt or lightning-shaft of Zeus, but later placed among the stars. The serpent is certainly the sign or totem, through the ages, of healing and of that final healing when we slough off, for the last time, our encumbering flesh or skin. The serpent is symbol of death, as we know, but also of resurrection.

There was no picture of this. Ezra said airily, "The thistle just goes with it." I do not think he actually identified the thistle in connection with the serpent, but in any case it was he who first gave me the idea of Asklepios, the "blameless physician," in that connection. I found this design later but only once and in only one place. I was with Frances Josepha and her mother on our first trip "abroad." This was the summer of 1911. We went from New York to Havre, then by boat up the Seine to Paris. "Here it is," I said on one of our first visits to the galleries of the Louvre, "quick," as if it might vanish like the original "brick." It was a small signet-ring in a case of Graeco-Roman or Hellenistic seals and signets. Under the glass, set in a row with other seal-rings, was a little grey-agate oval. It was a small ring with rather fragile setting, as far as one could judge, but the design was unmistakable. On the right side, as in the original, was the coiled, upright serpent; on the left, an exquisitely chased stalk, with the spiny double leaf and the flower-head, our thistle. I have never found this design anywhere else; there are serpents enough and heraldic thistles but I have not found the two in combination, though I have leafed over reference books from time to time, at odd moments, or glanced over classic coin designs or talismans just "in case." I never found my serpent and thistle in any illustrated volume of Greek or Ptolemaic design or in any odd corner on an actual Greek pottery jar or Etruscan vase, but through the years as I stopped off in Paris, on cross-continental journeys, I went back to assure myself that I had not, at any rate, "dreamt" the signet-ring. There it was; it was always in the same place, under the glass, in the frame, with the small slip of faded paper with a letter or a group of letters and a number. Once I even went to the length of purchasing the special catalogue that dealt with this section, hoping for some detail, but there was the briefest mention of "my" little ring; I read, "intaglio or signet-ring of Graeco-Roman or Hellenistic design," and a suitable approximate date. That was all.

SIGNET—as from sign, a mark, token, proof;
signet—the privy seal, a seal; signet-ring—
a ring with a signet or private seal; sign-
manual—the royal signature, usually only
the initials of the sovereign's name. (I have
used my initials H. D. consistently as my
writing signet or sign-manual, though it is
only, at this very moment, as I check up on
the word "signet" in my Chambers's English Dictionary that I realize that my writing signature has anything remotely suggesting sovereignty or the royal manner.)
Sign again—a word, gesture, symbol or
mark, intended to signify something else.
Sign again—(medical) a symptom, (astro-
nomical) one of the 12 parts of the Zodiac.
Again sign—to attach a signature to, and
sign-post—a direction post; all from the
French, *signe,* and Latin, *signum.* And as
I write that last word, there flashes into my
mind the associated *in hoc signum* or rather,
it must be *in hoc signo* and *vinces.*

THERE WAS A HANDFUL of old rings in a corner of one of the Professor's cases and I thought of my signet-ring at the galleries of the Louvre in Paris, but I did not speak of it to the Professor then or later, and though I felt curious about the rings at the time, I did not suggest his opening the door of the case and showing them to me. He had taken up one of the figures on his desk. He was holding it in his hand and looking at me. This, I surmised, was the image that he thought would interest me most. There was an ivory Indian figure in the centre; the objects were arranged symmetrically and I wondered if the seated Vishnu (I think it was) belonged there in the centre by right of precedence or preference or because of its shape. Though I realized the beautiful quality and design of the ivory, I was seeing it rather abstractly; the subject itself did not especially appeal to me. Serpent-heads rose like flower-petals to form a dome or tent over the head of the seated image; possibly it was seated on a flower or leaf; the effect of the whole was of a half-flower, cut lengthwise, the figure taking the place or producing the effect of a stamen-cluster or oval seed-pod, in the centre.

Only when you came close, you saw the little image and the symmetrical dome-like background of the snakes' heads. It is true, these snake-heads suggested, each, a half-*S*, which might have recalled the scroll pattern of the inverted *S* or incomplete question-mark in the picture series on the wall of the bedroom in the Greek island of Corfu of that spring of 1920. But I did not make this comparison then or afterwards to the Professor, and I felt a little uneasy before the extreme beauty of this carved Indian ivory which compelled me, yet repelled me, at the same time.

I did not always know if the Professor's excursions with me into the other room were by way of distraction, actual social occasions, or part of his plan. Did he want to find out how I would react to certain ideas embodied in these little statues, or how deeply I felt the dynamic *idea* still implicit in spite of the fact that ages or aeons of time had flown over many of them? Or did he mean simply to imply that he wanted to share his treasures with me, those tangible shapes before us that yet suggested the intangible and vastly more fascinating treasures of his own mind? Whatever his idea, I wanted then, as at other times, to meet him half-way; I wanted to return, in as unobtrusive a way as possible, the courtesy that was so subtly offered me. If it was a *game*, a sort of roundabout way of finding out something that perhaps my unconscious guard or censor was anxious to keep from him, well, I would do my best to play this game, this guessing game—or whatever it was. So, as the ivory had held my attention and perhaps (I did not know) it was especially valued by him, as it held the centre place on his imposing desk (that seemed placed there, now I come to think of it, almost like a high altar, in the Holy of Holies), I said, realizing my slight aversion to this exquisite work of art, "That ivory—what is it? It's Indian obviously. It's very beautiful."

He said, barely glancing at the lovely object, "It was sent to me by a group of my Indian students." He added, "On the whole, I think my Indian students have reacted in the least satisfactory way to my teaching." So much for India, so much for his Indian students. This was not his favourite, this Oriental, passionate yet cold abstraction. He had chosen something else. It was a smallish object, judging by the place left empty, my end of the semicircle, made by the symmetrical arrangement of the Gods (or the Goods) on his table.

"*This* is my favourite," he said. He held the object toward me. I took it in my hand. It was a little bronze statue, helmeted, clothed to the foot in carved robe with the upper incised chiton or peplum. One hand was extended as if holding a staff or rod. "She is perfect," he said, "*only she has lost her spear.*" I did not say anything. He knew that I loved Greece. He knew that I loved Hellas. I stood looking at Pallas Athené, she whose winged attribute was Niké, Victory, or she stood wingless, Niké A-pteros in the old days, in the little temple to your right as you climb the steps to the Propylaea on the Acropolis at Athens. He too had climbed those steps once, he had told me, for the briefest survey of the glory that was Greece. Niké A-pteros, she was called, the Wingless Victory, for Victory could never, would never fly away from Athens.

52

SHE HAS LOST HER SPEAR. He might have been talking Greek. The beautiful tone of his voice had a way of taking an English phrase or sentence out of its context (out of the associated context, you might say, of the whole language) so that, although he was speaking English without a perceptible trace of accent, yet he was speaking a foreign language. The tone of his voice, the singing quality that so subtly permeated the texture of the spoken word, made that spoken word live in another dimension, or take on another colour, as if he had dipped the grey web of conventionally woven thought and with it, conventionally *spoken* thought, into a vat of his own brewing—or held a strip of that thought, ripped from the monotonous faded and outworn texture of the language itself, into the bubbling cauldron of his own mind in order to draw it forth dyed blue or scarlet, a new colour to the old grey mesh, a scrap of thought, even a cast-off rag, that would become hereafter a pennant, a standard, a *sign* again, to indicate a direction or, fluttering aloft on a pole, to lead an army.

And on the other hand, when he said, *she is perfect*, he meant not only that the little bronze statue was a perfect symbol, made in man's image (in woman's, as it happened), to be venerated as a projection of abstract thought, Pallas Athené, born without human or even without divine mother, sprung full-armed from the head of her father, our-father, Zeus, Theus or God; he meant as well, this little piece of metal you hold in your hand (look at it) is priceless really, it is *perfect*, a prize, a find of the best period of Greek art, the classic period in its most concrete expression, before it became top-heavy with exterior trappings and ornate detail. This is a perfect specimen of Greek art, produced at the moment when the archaic abstraction became humanized but not yet over-humanized.

"She is perfect," he said and he meant that the image was of the accepted classic period, Periclean or just pre-Periclean; he meant that there was no scratch or flaw, no dent in the surface or stain on the metal, no fold of the peplum worn down or erosed away. He was speaking as an ardent lover of art and as an art-collector. He was speaking in a double sense, it is true, but he was speaking of value, the actual intrinsic value of the piece; like a Jew, he was assessing its worth; the blood of Abraham, Isaac and Jacob ran in his veins. He knew his material pound, his pound of flesh, if you will, but this pound of flesh was a *pound of spirit* between us, something tangible, to be weighed and measured, to be weighed in the balance and—pray God—not to be found wanting!

53

HE HAD SAID, he had dared to say that the dream had its worth and value in translatable terms, not the dream merely of a Pharaoh or a Pharaoh's butler, not the dream merely of the favourite child of Israel, not merely Joseph's dream or Jacob's dream of a symbolic ladder, not the dream only of the Cumaean Sybil of Italy or the Delphic Priestess of ancient Greece, but the dream of everyone, everywhere. He had dared to say that the dream came from an unexplored depth in man's consciousness and that this unexplored depth ran like a great stream or ocean underground, and the vast depth of that ocean was the same vast depth that to-day, as in Joseph's day, overflowing in man's small consciousness, produced inspiration, madness, creative idea or the dregs of the dreariest symptoms of mental unrest and disease. He had dared to say that it was the same ocean of universal consciousness, and even if not stated in so many words, he had dared to imply that this consciousness proclaimed all men one; all nations and races met in the universal world of the dream; and he had dared to say that the dream-symbol could be interpreted; its language, its imagery were common to the whole race, not only of the living but of those ten thousand years dead. The picture-writing, the hieroglyph of the dream, was the common property of the whole race; in the dream, man, as at the beginning of time, spoke a universal language, and man, meeting in the universal understanding of the unconscious or the subconscious, would forgo barriers of time and space, and man, understanding man, would save mankind.

54

WITH PRECISE Jewish instinct for the particular in the general, for the personal in the impersonal or universal, for the *material* in the abstract, he had dared to plunge into the unexplored depth, first of his own unconscious or subconscious being. From it, he dredged, as samples of his theories, his own dreams, exposing them as serious discoveries, facts, with cause and effect, beginning and end, often showing from even the most trivial dream sequence the powerful dramatic impact that projected it. He took the events of the day preceding the night of the dream, the dream-day as he called it; he unravelled from the mixed con-

ditions and contacts of the ordinary affairs
of life the particular thread that went on
spinning its length through the substance of
the mind, the *buried* mind, the sleeping, the
unconscious or subconscious mind. The
thread so eagerly identified as part of the
pattern, part of some commonplace or some
intricate or intimate matter of the waking
life, would as likely as not be lost, at the
precise moment when, identified, it showed
its shimmering or its drab dream-substance.
The sleeping mind was not one, not all
equally sleeping; part of the unconscious
mind would become conscious at a least expected moment; this part of the dreaming
mind that laid traps or tricked the watcher
or slammed doors on the scene or the unravelling tapestry of the dream sequence he
called the Censor; it was guardian at the
gates of the underworld, like the dog Cer-
berus, of Hell.

55

IN THE DREAM MATTER were Heaven and
Hell, and he spared himself and his first
avidly curious, mildly shocked readers
neither. He did not spare himself or his

later growing public, but others he spared. He would break off a most interesting dream-narrative, to explain that personal matter, concerning *not himself*, had intruded. *Know thyself*, said the ironic Delphic oracle, and the sage or priest who framed the utterance knew that to know yourself in the full sense of the words was to know everybody. *Know thyself*, said the Professor, and plunging time and again, he amassed that store of intimate revelation contained in his impressive volumes. But to *know thyself*, to set forth the knowledge, brought down not only a storm of abuse from high-placed doctors, psychologists, scientists and other accredited intellectuals the world over, but made his very name almost a by-word for illiterate quips, unseemly jokes and general ridicule.

56

MAYBE HE LAUGHED at the jokes, I don't know. His beautiful mouth seemed always slightly smiling, though his eyes, set deep and slightly asymmetrical under the domed forehead (with those furrows cut by a master chisel), were unrevealing. His eyes did not speak to me. I can not even say that they were sad eyes. If at a moment of distress—as when I went to him that day when all the doors in Vienna were closed and the streets empty—there came that pause that sometimes fell between us, he, sensing some almost unbearable anxiety and tension in me, would break this spell with some kindly old-world courtesy, some question: What had I been reading? Did I find the books I wanted in the library his wife's sister had recommended? Of course—if I wanted any of his books at any time— Had I heard again from Bryher, from my daughter? Had I heard lately from America?

I would have taken the hour-glass in my hand and set it the other way round so that the sands of his life would have as many years to run forward as now ran backward. Or I would have slipped through a secret door—only I would have the right to do this—and entreat a kindly Being. (Only I could do this, for my gift must be something different.) I would change my years for his; it would not be as generous a number as I could have wished for him, yet it would make a difference. Perhaps there would be 20 years, even 30 years left in my hour-glass. "Look," I would say to this kindly Being, "those two on your shelf

there—just make the slightest alteration of
the hour-glasses. Put H. D. in the place of
Sigmund Freud (I will still have a few years
left in which to tidy up my not very important affairs). It's not too much to ask
of you. And it can be done. Someone did it
or offered to do it in a play once. It was a
Greek play, wasn't it? A woman—I don't
remember her name—offered her years in
exchange to—someone else for—something.
What was it? There was Hercules or Her-
akles and a struggle with Death. Was the
play called *Alcestis*? I wonder. And of
course, one of those 3 must have written it
—there they are on the top of the Professor's case, to the right of the wide-opened
double door that leads into his inner sanctum. Aeschylus? Sophocles? Euripides?
Who wrote the *Alcestis*? But it doesn't
really matter who wrote it, for the play is
going on now—at any rate we are acting it,
the old Professor and I. The old Professor
doubles the part. He is Hercules struggling
with Death and he is the beloved, about to
die. Moreover he himself, in his own charac-
ter, has made the dead live, has summoned
a host of dead and dying children from the
living tomb."

57

WHEN I SAID TO HIM one day that time went too quickly (did he or didn't he feel that?) he struck a semi-comic attitude, he threw his arm forward as if ironically addressing an invisible presence or an imaginary audience. "*Time,*" he said. The word was uttered in his inimitable, two-edged manner; he seemed to defy the creature, the abstraction; into that one word, he seemed to pack a store of contradictory emotions; there was irony, entreaty, defiance, with a vague, tender pathos. It seemed as if the word was surcharged, an explosive that might, at any minute, go off. (Many of his words did, in a sense, explode, blasting down prisons, useless dykes and dams, bringing down landslides, it is true, but opening up mines of hidden treasure.) "*Time,*" he said again, more quietly, and then, "*time gallops.*"

"Time gallops withal." I wonder if he knew that he was quoting Shakespeare? Though the exact application of Rosalind's elaborate quip about Time hardly seems appropriate. "Who doth he gallop withal?" asks Orlando. And Rosalind answers, "with a thief to the gallows; for though he go as softly as foot can fall, he thinks himself too soon there." But a thief certainly; in a greater dramatic tradition, he had stolen fire, like Prometheus, from heaven.

58

STOP THIEF! But nothing could stop him, once he started unearthing buried treasures (he called it striking oil). And anyhow, wasn't it his own? Hadn't he found it? But *stop thief*, they shouted or worse. He was nonchalantly unlocking vaults and caves, taking down the barriers that generations had carefully set up against their hidden motives, their secret ambitions, their suppressed desires. *Stop thief!* Admit, however, that what he offered as treasure, this revelation that he seemed to value, was poor stuff, trash indeed, ideas that a ragpicker would pass over in disdain, old junk stored in the attic, put away, forgotten, not even worth the trouble of cutting up for firewood, cumbersome at that, difficult to move, and moreover if you started to move one unwieldly cumbersome idea, you might dislodge the whole cart-load of junk; it had been there such a long time, it was almost part of the wall and the attic ceiling

of the house of life. *Stop thief!* But why,
after all, stop him? His so-called discoveries
were patently ridiculous. Time gallops
withal . . . with a thief to the gallows. And
give a man enough rope—we have heard
somewhere—and he will hang himself!

59

HE WAS A LITTLE SURPRISED at the outburst.
He had not thought that detached and
lofty practitioners and men of science
could be so angry at what was, after all,
chapter and verse, a contribution to a
branch of abstract thought, applied to medical science. He had worked with the famous Dr. Charcot in Paris. There are other
names that figure in the historical account
given us by Professor Freud himself in his
short *Autobiographical Study*. We have
the names of doctors, famous specialists,
who gave an idea to Freud; we have Freud
himself impartially dividing honours between Breuer (or whoever it happens to
be) and Freud. We have Freud himself giving Freud credit for the discovery of the
cocaine anaesthesia attributed to Koller.
But when I asked the analyst Walter

Schmideberg when and how the Professor happened on the idea that led to his linking up neurotic states of megalomania and aggrandisement with, in certain instances, fantasies of youth and childhood, he answered me, correctly and conventionally; he said that Freud did not happen on ideas. I wonder? And said I wondered. But Mr. Schmideberg repeated what already, of course, I was supposed to know, that the whole established body of work was founded on accurate and accumulated data of scientific observation. That is not what I asked. I wanted to know at what exact moment, and in what manner, there came that flash of inspiration, that thing that clicked, that sounded, that shouted in the inner Freud mind, heart or soul, *this is it*.

But things don't happen like that. Or do they? At least we are free to wonder. We ourselves are free to imagine, to reconstruct, to *see* even, as in a play or film, those characters, in their precise setting, the Paris of that period, 1885. Dr. Charcot was concerned with hysteria and neurotics this side of the border-line. That border-line, it is true, was of necessity but vaguely indicated; there were hysterics, neurotics on this side and the actual insane on the other but there was a wide gap for all that, an un-

explored waste-land, a no-man's land between them. At least there was a no-man's
land; at least there were cases that not so
very long ago would have been isolated
as insane that now came under a milder
rule, the kingdom of hysteria. The world
of medical knowledge had made vast strides
for there was still a memory in the minds
of the older generations of eye-witness
tales of a time, here in this very city, when
the inmates of the insane asylums were fas-
tened with chains, like wild beasts, to the
walls or to iron rails or stakes; moreover,
the public was admitted at stated intervals
to view the wild animals in the course of a
holiday tour of the city. That time was
past, not so very long past, it is true, yet
past, due to the humanitarian efforts of the
preceding generation of scientists and doctors. They had progressed certainly. And
our Professor could, in point of fact, have
visited the more "modern" foundations of
that time and place. Paris? He was a
stranger. 1870 was by no means forgotten.
He had seen the fangs of the pack during
his student days. He writes of his early
days at the University in Vienna, "Above
all, I found that I was expected to feel myself inferior and alien because I was a Jew."
He adds, "I refused absolutely to do the

first of these things." But there were others, here in Paris, inferiors, aliens certainly, who dwelt apart from their fellow-men, not chained, though still (in more human surroundings) segregated, separated, in little rooms, we may conclude, or cells with bars before the windows or doors. An improvement certainly. They too "refused absolutely" to feel themselves inferior. On the contrary. These were special cases, but there was the great crowd at large, under observation at the Salpêtrière. But among the hysterical cases under Charcot's observation and the insane of the young Freud's own private consideration, there were incidents unnoted or minimized by the various doctors and observers, which yet held matter worth grave consideration. He noted how the disconnected sequence of the apparently unrelated actions of certain of the patients yet suggested a sort of order, followed a pattern like the broken sequence of events in a half-remembered dream. Dream? Was the dream then, in its turn, projected or suggested by events in the daily life, was the dream the counter-coin side of madness or was madness a waking dream? There was an odd element of tragedy sometimes, something not always wholly on the physical or sordid material level. It was Hell, of course. But these people in Hell sometimes bore strange resemblance to things he had remembered, things he had read about, old Kings in old countries, women broken by wars, and enslaved, distorted children.

There were bars before some of the cells (in this scene built up purely from our own intuitive imagination), yet these cages sometimes presented scenes as from a play. Caesar strutted there. There Hannibal— Hannibal? Why Hannibal? As a boy he himself had worshipped Hannibal, imagined himself in the rôle of world-conquerer. But every boy at some time or another strutted with imaginary sword and armour. *Every boy?* This man, this Caesar, who flung his toga over his arm with a not altogether unauthentic gesture, might simply be living out some childish fantasy. If he could examine the patient in suitable surroundings—but the patient shouted *et tu Brute* and became violent at any suggestion of approach or friendly contact. If he could have interviewed this Caesar a few years back—he had been a man of some prominence at one time—he might have been able to worm out of him the secret of his Caesar mania. The mind was clouded now but there was no report in this case of actual tissue decay or the usual physical symptoms that end inevitably in madness. Caesar? Hannibal? These were outstanding recognizable historical personages. But were these the entities that caused this—*fixation* was a word not yet coined in this connection. This man was acting a part, Caesar. Caesar? He himself, as a child, enacted a similar rôle, Hannibal. But was it Hannibal? Was it Caesar? Was it—? Well, yes—it might be—how odd. Yes—it could be! It might be this man's father now that he was impersonating—wasn't the father the Caesar, the conqueror, the symbol of power, the Czar, Kaiser, the King in the child's kingdom—admittedly small but to the child of vast world-wide importance, the world to him, his home. The whole world for a child is its home, its father, mother, brothers, sisters and so on—its school later and friends from other "kingdoms." Why yes—how clear it all was—this Caesar now? How had it come about? There must be something behind this collapse not noted in the record of the patient's physical and even mental conditions and symptoms. There must be something else behind many of these cases here and at the Salpêtrière—not all of them—but some of them—and other cases. . . . There must be something behind the whole build-up of present-day medical science—there must be something further on or deeper down— there must be something that would reveal the secrets of these states of glorified personality and other states and conditions— there must be something. . . . Why, Hannibal! There is Caesar behind bars—here is Hannibal, here am I, Sigmund Freud, watching Caesar behind bars. But it was Caesar who was conqueror—was he? I came, I saw, I conquered—yes, I will conquer. I will. I, Hannibal—not Caesar. I, the despised Carthaginian, I, the enemy of Rome. I, Hannibal. So you see, I, Sigmund Freud, myself standing here, a favourite and gifted, admit it, student of Dr. Charcot, in no way to all appearances deranged or essentially peculiar, true to my own orbit—*true to my own orbit?* True to my own orbit, my childhood fantasies of Hannibal, my identification with Hannibal, the Carthaginian (Jew, not Roman)—I, Sigmund Freud, understand this Caesar. I, Hannibal!

And Caesar's wife too (if we may continue our build-up of this purely imaginative sequence of cause and effect), there is Caesar's wife to be considered. This particular lady was not even an out-patient of this particular institution, but she might soon be. She was found lingering in the waiting room, after the others had left. She was always demanding interviews with the doctors and the superintendent himself, getting in everyone's way. It was becoming quite a feature with the institution, the superintendent had left special orders that he was not to be disturbed, he had been compelled to deny her the last private interview she demanded; the famous specialist was overworked, there was too much to be done here, everywhere, trying personal entanglements must be avoided at all costs. *Personal entanglements?* But this good lady would be the first to decry any such shadow of design on her part. But wasn't that her trouble? She had been devoted to her husband, the separation was affecting her, she herself seemed on the verge of a serious breakdown. That was only natural, wasn't it, under the tragic circumstances? But this sort of suppressed neurotic symptom—*symptom?* This sort of separation between two people long married and devoted, might have serious repercussions, actually throw the whole nervous system out of gear, unbalance the delicately adjusted mechanism of the mind itself. Her worry had worn on her—poor woman—and no wonder. Someone should look after her.

But she was not even an out-patient, it wasn't their business to probe into the personal affairs of the patients' wives and families. *Affairs?* Caesar's wife? Yes, she was Caesar's wife, obviously above suspicion, a conventional woman yet a woman of the world. Such things had happened before. Where was his thought taking him? There had been other cases here—that girl whose happiness at the news of her husband's possible return from Algiers after a long absence had so improved her condition that Dr. Charcot, consulted in this instance, had himself suggested her leaving the hospital for a time. Her health, it was reported, had improved after her return to her husband, but *if her husband went away again would her symptoms return?*

60

THIS OBVIOUSLY IS NOT an historical account of the preliminary steps that led to the establishment of a new branch of psychological research and a new form of healing called psychoanalysis. The actual facts are accessible to any serious student of Professor Freud's work. But it seems to me it

might have been through some such process of inner reasoning that the theme
opened. The *theme?* I write the word and
wonder why I write it. It seemed to me to
suggest music—yes, musical terms do seem
relevant to the curious and original process
of the Professor's intuitive reasoning that
led up to, developed, amplified, simplified
the first astonishing findings of the young
Viennese doctor whom the diagnoses of his
elders and betters had not always satisfied.
It was not only that the young Sigmund
Freud was astute, methodical, conscientious, subtle, clever, original—though he
was all these. It was not only that he came
from a race that had venerated learning and
(like the Arabs) had preserved, in spite of
repeated persecutions, a singular *feeling*
for medicine, along with mathematics and
certain forms of abstract philosophy and
poetry, at a time when (as now) the liberal
and applied arts seemed overshadowed
with the black wing of man's growing
power of destruction and threat of racial
separateness. He stood alone and we may
imagine that he was singularly proud,
though of so genial a nature, so courteous
a manner and so delicate a wit; he was easy
to get on with, he could discourse delight-
fully on any subject, at any time, with

anybody. But what was it about him? His appearance, his habits, his way of life were conventional enough; even his worst enemies could find nothing to criticize about his private life; he was strictly correct, almost orthodox, you might say.

The point was that for all his amazing originality, he was drawing from a source so deep in human consciousness that the outer rock or shale, the accumulation of hundreds or thousands of years of casual, slack or even wrong or evil thinking, had all but sealed up the original spring or well-head. He called it striking oil, but others—long ago—had dipped into that same spring. They called it "a well of living water" in the old days, or simply the "still waters." The Professor spoke of this source of inspiration in terms of oil. It focused the abstraction, made it concrete, a modern business symbol. Although it was obvious that he was speaking of a vague, vast abstraction, he used a common, almost a commonplace, symbol for it. He used the idiom or slang of the counting-house, of Wall Street, a business man's concrete definite image for a successful run of luck or hope of success in the if-we-should-strike-oil or old-so-and-so-has-struck-oil-again manner. "I struck oil but there is enough left for 50, for 100 years or more." It is difficult to imagine the Professor saying solemnly, "I drew by right of inheritance from the great source of inspiration of Israel and the Psalmist—Jeremiah, some might call me. I stumbled on a well of living water, the river of life. It ran muddy or bright. It was blocked by fallen logs, some petrified—and an accumulation of decaying leaves and branches. I saw the course of the river and how it ran, and I, personally, cleared away a bit of rubbish, so that at least a small section of the river should run clear. There is a lot yet to be done—for a hundred years or more—so that all men, all nations, may gather together, understanding in the end. . . ." But no, that was not the Professor's way of talking. "I struck oil" suggests business enterprise. We visualize stark uprights and skeleton-like steel cages, like unfinished Eiffel Towers. And there are many, I have reason to know, who think of the whole method or system of psychoanalysis in some such terms, a cage, some mechanical construction set up in an arid desert, to trap the unwary, and if there is "oil" to be inferred, the "oil" goes to someone else; there are astute doctors who "squeeze you dry" with their exorbitant fees for prolonged and expensive treat-

ments. A tiresome subject at best—have
nothing to do with it—it's worn out, dated;
true, it was fashionable enough among the
young intellectuals after the first World
War but they turned out a dreary lot and
who, after all, has heard of any of them
since?

61

TIRESOME INDEED! So is Aeschylus tiresome
to most people, so is Sophocles, so is Plato
and that old Socrates with his tedious matter and his more than tedious manner. The
Socratic method? That was a business of
egging on an intellectual contestant, almost
in the manner of a fencer with pin-pricks
—wasn't it?—or sword-pricks of prodding
questions that would eventually bring the
debatable matter to a head, so that the fight
could be open and above-board, unless the
rival were slain in the preliminary clash of
intellectual steel. There was something of
that in the Professor's method of analytic
treatment, but there was a marked difference. The question must be propounded
by the protagonist himself, he must dig it
out from its buried hiding-place, he himself

must find the question before it could be
answered.

62

HE HIMSELF must clear away his own rubbish, before his particular stream, his personal life, could run clear of obstruction
into the great river of humanity, hence to
the sea of superhuman perfection, the "Absolute" as Socrates or Plato called it.

63

BUT WE ARE here to-day in a city of ruin, a
world ruined, it might seem, almost past re-
demption. We must forgo a flight from
reality into the green pastures or the cool
recesses of the Academe; though those pastures and those gardens have outlasted many
ruined cities and threat of world ruin; we
are not ready for discussion of the Absolute, Absolute Beauty, Absolute Truth,
Absolute Goodness. We have rested in the
pastures, we have wandered beside those
still waters, we have sensed the fragrance

of the myrtle thickets beyond distant hedges, and the groves of flowering citrons. *Kennst du das Land?* Oh yes, Professor, I know it very well. But I am remembering the injunction you laid upon me and I am thinking of my fellow-pupil whose place you say I have taken, my brother-in-arms, the Flying Dutchman, who, intellectually gifted beyond the ordinary run of man, endowed with Eastern islands and plantations, trained to a Western discipline of mind and body, yet flew too high and flew too quickly.

64

THE PROFESSOR is speaking to me very seriously. This is in his study in Vienna a few weeks after I had first begun my work there. "I am asking only one thing of you," he said. Even as I write the words, I have the same sense of anxiety, of tension, of imminent responsibility that I had at that moment. What can he possibly be going to say? What can he ask me to do? Or not to do? More likely a *shalt not* than a demand for some specific act or course of action. His manner was serious yet kindly. Yet in spite of that or because of that, I felt like a child, summoned to my father's study or my mother's sewing-room or told by a teacher to wait in after school, after the others had left, for those "few words" that were for myself alone. *Stop thief!* What had I done? What was I likely to do? "I ask only one thing of you children"—my mother's very words.

65

FOR THE PROFESSOR is standing in his study. The Professor is asking only one thing of me. I was right in my premonition, it is a *shalt not.* He is asking something of me, confiding in me, treating me in his courteous, subtle way as an intellectual equal. He is very firm about this, however, and he is patiently explaining it to me. "Of course, you understand" is the offhand way in which he offers me, from time to time, some rare discovery, some priceless finding, or "Perhaps you may feel differently" as if my feelings, my discoveries, were on a par with his own. He does not lay down the law, only this once—this one law. He says, "Please, never—I mean, never at any time, in any circumstance, endeavour to defend me, if and when you hear abusive remarks made about me and my work."

He explained it carefully. He might have been giving a lesson in geometry or demonstrating the inevitable course of a disease once the virus has entered the system. At this point, he seemed to indicate (as if there were a chart of a fever patient, pinned on the wall before us), at the least suggestion that you may be about to begin a counter-argument in my defence, the anger or the frustration of the assailant will be driven deeper. You will do no good to the detractor by mistakenly beginning a logical defence. You will drive the hatred or the fear or the prejudice in deeper. You will do no good to yourself, for you will only expose your own feelings—I take for granted that you have deep feelings about my discoveries, or you would not be here. You will do no good to me and my work, for antagonism, once taking hold, can not be rooted out from above the surface, and it thrives, in a way, on heated argument and digs in deeper. The only way to extract the fear or prejudice would be from within, from below, and as naturally this type of prejudiced or frightened mind would dodge any hint of a suggestion of psychoanalytic treatment or even, put it, study and research along these lines, you can not get at the root of the trouble. Every word, spoken in my defence, I mean, to already prejudiced individuals, serves to drive the root in deeper. If the matter is ignored, the attacker may forgo his anger—or in time, even, his unconscious mind may find another object on which to fix its tentacles. . . .

This was the gist of the matter. In our talks together he rarely used any of the now rather overworked technical terms, invented by himself and elaborated on by the growing body of doctors, psychologists and nerve specialists who form the somewhat formidable body of the International Psycho-Analytical Association. When, on one occasion, I was endeavouring to explain a matter in which my mind tugged two ways, I said, "I suppose you would say it was a matter of ambivalence?" And as he did not answer me, I said, "Or do you say am-*bi*-valence? I don't know whether it's pronounced ambi-*valence* or am-*bi*-valence." The Professor's arm shot forward as it did on those occasions when he wished to stress a finding or focus my attention to some point in hand; he said, in his curiously casual ironical manner, "Do you know, I myself have always wondered. I often wish that I could find someone to explain these matters to me."

66

THERE WAS SO MUCH to be explained, so little time in which to do it. My serpent-and-thistle motive, for instance, or *Leitmotiv*, I had almost written. It was a sign, a symbol certainly—it must have been—but even if I had found another seal-ring like the one I saw in Paris, among that handful of old rings in the corner of the shelf in the other room, it wouldn't have proved anything and might have led us too far afield in a discussion or reconstruction of cause and effect, which might indeed have included priceless treasures, gems and jewels, among the so-called findings of the unconscious mind revealed by the dream-content or associated thought and memory, yet have side-tracked the issue in hand. My serpent and thistle—what did it remind me of? There was Aaron's rod, of course, which when flung to the ground turned into a living reptile. Reptile? Aaron's rod, if I am not mistaken, was originally the staff of

Moses. There was Moses in the bulrushes, "our" dream and "our" Princess. There was the ground, cursed by God because Adam and Eve had eaten of the Fruit of the Tree. Henceforth, it would bring forth thorns and thistles—thorns, thistles, the words conjure up the same scene, the barren unproductive waste or desert. *Do men gather grapes of thorns, or figs of thistles?* Another question, another question-mark, a half-*S*, the other way round, *S* for *s*eal, *s*ymbol, *s*erpent certainly, *s*ignet, Sigmund.

67

SIGMUND, the singing voice; no, it is Siegmund really, the victorious mouth or voice or utterance. There was Victory, our sign on the wall, our hieroglyph, our writing. There was the tiny bronze, his favourite among the semicircle of the Gods or as "other people read: Goods" on his table. There was Niké, Victory, and Niké A-pteros, the Wingless Victory, for Victory could never, would never fly away from Athens. There was Athens, a city set on a hill; hill, mountain; there was Berggasse, the hill, *Berg,* and the path or street

or way, *gasse.* There were designs, weren't
there, of acanthus leaves to crown upright
Corinthian capitals? And the Latin *acanthus,* and the related Greek word *akantha,*
is thorn or prickle. There were patterns,
decorative hieroglyphs of acanthus leaves,
a very classic symbol; and there was a
crown, we have been told, in the end, of
thorns.

68

BUT TO OUR LITTLE abridged Greek Lexi-
con, to verify *akantha.* Yes—as from *aké,* a
point, edge, hence a prickly plant, thistle;
also a thorny tree. *A thorny tree.* Was our
thistle the sign or sigil of all thorny trees?
Perhaps even of that singularly prickly
Tree of the Knowledge of Good and Evil
with its attendant Serpent. There were,
and are, many varieties of serpents. There
was, among many others, that serpent of
Wisdom that crouched at the feet of the
goddess Athené and was one of her attri-
butes, like the spear (*aké,* a point) she held
in her hand—though we can not be sure
that it was a spear that the Professor's perfect little bronze once held in her hand. It
might have been a rod or staff.

69

THY ROD AND THY STAFF. In England, our
American goldenrod, that runs riot in the
late-summer fields and along every lane
and at the edge of every strip of woodland,
is cultivated in tidy clumps in gardens, and
is called Aaron's rod. The goldenrod
brings us to the Golden Bough; it was to
Plato that Meleager, in the Greek Anthol-
ogy, attributed the golden bough, ever
shining with its own light. And the Professor, one winter day, offered me a little
branch. He explained that his son in the
South of France had posted (or sent by
some acquaintance returning to Vienna
from the Midi) a box of oranges, and some
branches with leaves were among them.
He thought I might like this. I took the
branch, a tiny tree in itself, with its cluster
of golden fruit. I thanked the Professor. At
least, I murmured some platitude, "How
lovely—how charming of you" or some
such. Did he know, did he ever know, or
did he ever not-know, what I was thinking? I did not say what I had no time to
formulate into words—or if I had had time
for other than a superficial "How lovely—
how perfectly charming," I could not have

trusted myself to say the words. They were there. They were singing. They went on singing like an echo of an echo in a shell —very far away yet very near—the very shell substance of my outer ear and the curled involuted or convoluted shell skull, and inside the skull, the curled, intricate, hermit-like mollusc, the brain-matter itself. Thoughts are things—sometimes they are songs. I did not have to recall the words, I had not written them. Another mollusc in a hard cap of bone or shell had projected these words. There was a song set to them, that still another singing skull had fashioned. No, not Schumann's music—lovely as it is—there was a song we sang as school-children, another setting to the words. And even the words sing themselves without music, so it does not matter that I have not been able to identify the "tune" as we lilted it. *Kennst du das Land?*

70

Kennst du das Land, wo die Zitronen blühn?

THE WORDS RETURN with singular freshness and poignancy, as I, after this long time of waiting, am able to remember without unbearable terror and overwhelming heart-break those sessions in Vienna. The war closed on us, before I had time to sort out, relive and reassemble the singular series of events and dreams that belonged in historical time, to the 1914–1919 period. I wanted to dig down and dig out, root out my personal weeds, strengthen my purpose, reaffirm my beliefs, canalize my energies, and I seized on the unexpected chance of working with Professor Freud himself. I could never have thought it possible to approach him, nor even have thought of inquiring if it were possible, if it had not been for Dr. Sachs's suggestion. I had had some fascinating, preliminary talks with Dr. Hanns Sachs in Berlin and wanted to go on with the work, but he was leaving for America. Dr. Sachs asked me if I would consider working with the Professor if he would take me? If he would take me? It seemed such a fantastic suggestion and to my mind highly unlikely that Freud himself would consider me as analysand or student. But *if* the Professor would accept me, I would have no choice whatever in the matter. I would go to him, of course.

71

I HAVE SAID earlier in these notes that the
Professor's explanations were too illuminating or too depressing. I meant that in
some strange way we had managed to get
at the root of things, *to-day, we have tunnelled very deep;* and in another still stranger way, we had approached the clearest
fountain-head of highest truth, as in the luminous *real* dream of the Princess and the
river which was in the realm of what is
known generally as the supernormal; it was
a scene or picture from those realms from
which the *illuminati* received their—"cre-
dentials" seems a strange word as I write it,
but it "wrote itself." My Princess picture
was one of an exquisite, endless sequence
from an *illuminated manuscript*, and has its
place in that category among books and
manuscripts; the dream, you may remember, I said in the beginning, varies like the
people we meet, like the books we read.
The books and the people merge in this
world of fantasy and imagination; none the
less we may differentiate with the utmost
felicity and fidelity between dreams and
the types of different fantasies; there are
the most trivial and tiresome dreams, the
newspaper class—but even there is, in an

old newspaper, sometimes a hint of eternal truth, or a quotation from a great man's speech or some tale of heroism, among the trashy and often sordid and trivial record of the day's events. The printed page varies, cheap news-print, good print, bad print, smudged and uneven print—there are the great letter words of an advertisement or the almost invisible pin-print; there are the huge capitals of a child's alphabet chart or building blocks; letters or ideas may run askew on the page, as it were; they may be purposeless; they may be stereotyped and not meant for "reading" but as a test, as for example the symmetrical letters that don't of necessity "spell" anything, on a doctor's or oculist's chart hung on the wall in an office or above a bed in a hospital. There are dreams or sequences of dreams that follow a line like a graph on a map or show a jagged triangular pattern, like a crack on a bowl that shows the bowl or vase may at any moment fall in pieces; we all know that almost invisible thread-line on the cherished glass butter-dish that predicts it will "come apart in me 'ands" sooner or later—sooner, more likely.

There are all these shapes, lines, graphs, the *hieroglyph of the unconscious*, and the Professor had first opened the field to the study of this vast, unexplored region. He himself—at least to me personally—deplored the tendency to *fix* ideas too firmly to set symbols, or to weld them inexorably. It is true that he himself started to decipher or decode the vast accumulation of the material of the unconscious mind; it was he who "struck oil" but the application of the "oil," what could or should be made of it, could not be entirely regulated or supervised by its original "promoter." He struck oil; certainly there was "something in it"; yes, a vast field for exploration and—alas—exploitation lay open. There were the immemorial Gods ranged in their semicircle on the Professor's table, that stood, as I have said, like the high altar in the Holy of Holies. There were those Gods, each the carved symbol of an idea or a deathless dream, that some people read: Goods.

72

THERE ARE THE WISE and the foolish virgins and their several lamps. *Thou anointest my head with oil*—the oil of understanding—and, indeed, *my cup runneth over*. But this purposes to be a personal reconstruction of intention and impression. I had begun my preliminary research in order to fortify and equip myself to face war when it came, and to help in some subsidiary way, if my training were sufficient and my aptitudes suitable, with war-shocked and war-shattered people. But my actual personal war-shock (1914-1919) did not have a chance. My sessions with the Professor were barely under way, before there were preliminary signs and symbols of the approaching ordeal. And the thing I primarily wanted to fight in the open, war, its cause and effect, with its inevitable aftermath of neurotic breakdown and related nerve disorders, was driven deeper. With the death-head swastika chalked on the pavement, leading to the Professor's very door, I must, in all decency, calm as best I could my own personal Phobia, my own personal little Dragon of war-terror, and with whatever power I could summon or command order him off, for the time being at any rate, back to his subterranean cavern.

There he growled and bit on his chains and was only loosed finally, when the full apocryphal terror of fire and brimstone, of whirlwind and flood and tempest, of the Biblical Day of Judgement and the Last Trump, became no longer abstractions, terrors too dreadful to be thought of, but things that were happening every day, every night, and at one time, at every hour of the day and night, to myself and my friends, and all the wonderful and all the drab and ordinary London people.

73

AND THE KINDLY Being whom I would have entreated had wafted the old Professor out of it. He had gone before the blast and bombing and fires had devastated this city; he was a handful of ashes, cherished in an urn or scattered among the grass and flowers in one of the Gardens of Remembrance, outside London. I suppose there must be a marble slab there on the garden wall or a little box in a niche beside a garden path. I have not even gone to look, to regard a familiar name with a date perhaps, and wander along a path, hedged with clipped yew or, more likely, fragrant dust-green lavender, and think of the Professor. For our Garden of Remembrance is somewhere else.

Kennst du das Land, wo die Zitronen blühn,
Im dunkeln Laub die Gold-Orangen glühn,
Ein sanfter Wind vom blauen Himmel weht,
Die Myrte still und hoch der Lorbeer steht,
Kennst du es wohl?
>   *Dahin! Dahin*
Möcht ich mit dir, o mein Geliebter, ziehn.

Kennst du das Haus? Auf Säulen ruht sein
>   *Dach,*
Es glänzt der Saal, es schimmert das Gemach,
Und Marmorbilder stehn und sehn mich an:
Was hat man dir, du armes Kind, getan?
Kennst du es wohl?
>   *Dahin! Dahin*
Möcht ich mit dir, o mein Beschützer, ziehn.

Kennst du den Berg und seinen Wolkensteg?
Das Maultier sucht im Nebel seinen Weg,
In Höhlen wohnt der Drachen alte Brut,
Es stürzt der Fels und über ihn die Flut;
Kennst du ihn wohl?
>   *Dahin! Dahin*
Geht unser Weg! o Vater, lass uns ziehn!

74

I HAVE SAID that these impressions must take me, rather than I take them. The first impression of all takes me back to the beginning, to my first session with the Professor. Paula has opened the door (though I did not then know that the pretty little Viennese maid was called Paula). She has divested me of my coat and made some welcoming remark which has slightly embarrassed me, as I am thinking English thoughts and only English words come to prompt me. She has shown me into the waiting-room with the lace-curtains at the window, with framed photographs of celebrities, some known personally to me; Dr. Havelock Ellis and Dr. Hanns Sachs gaze at me, familiar but a little distorted in their frames under the reflecting glass. There is the modest, treasured framed diploma from the small New England university, which I examined later, and the macabre, detailed, Düreresque symbolic drawing, a "Buried Alive" or of some such school of thought. I wait in this room. I know that Prof. Dr. Sigmund Freud will open the door which faces me. Although I know this and have been preparing for some months for this ordeal, I am, none the less, taken aback, surprised, shocked even, when the door opens. It seems to me, after my time of waiting, that he appears too suddenly.

Automatically, I walk through the door. It closes. Sigmund Freud does not speak. He is waiting for me to say something. I can not speak. I look round the room. A lover of Greek art, I am automatically taking stock of the room's contents. Pricelessly lovely objects are displayed here on the shelves to right, to left of me. I have been told about the Professor, his family, his way of life. I have heard certain personal anecdotes not available to the general readers of his books. I have heard him lovingly criticised by his adorers and soundly berated by his enemies. I know that he had a very grave recurrence of a former serious illness, some five years or so ago, and was again operated on for that particularly pernicious form of cancer of the mouth or tongue, and that by a miracle (to the amazement of the Viennese specialists) he recovered. It seems to me, in some curious way, that we were both "miraculously saved" for some purpose. But all this is a feeling, an atmosphere —something that I realize or perceive, but do not actually put into words or thoughts. I could not have said this even if I had, at that moment, realized it. I do know that it is a great privilege to be here, this I do actually realize. I am here because Dr. Sachs suggested my coming here and wrote the Professor about me. Dr. Sachs had talked lovingly about the Professor and, sometimes in gentle irony, had spoken of the "poor Frau Professor." But no one had told me that this room was lined with treasures. I was to greet the Old Man of the Sea, but no one had told me of the treasures he had salvaged from the sea-depth.

75

HE IS AT home here. He is part and parcel of these treasures. I have come a long way, I have brought nothing with me. He has his family, the tradition of an unbroken family, reaching back through this old heart of the Roman Empire, further into the Holy Land.

Ah, Psyche, from the regions which
Are Holy Land!

He is the infinitely old symbol, weighing the soul, Psyche, in the Balance. Does the Soul, passing the portals of life, entering the House of Eternity, greet the Keeper of the

Door? It seems so. I should have thought the Door-Keeper, at home beyond the threshold, might have greeted the shivering soul. Not so, the Professor. But waiting and finding that I would not or could not speak, he uttered. What he said—and I thought a little sadly—was, "You are the only person who has ever come into this room and looked at the things in the room before looking at me."

But worse was to come. A little lion-like creature came padding toward me—a lioness, as it happened. She had emerged from the inner sanctum or manifested from under or behind the couch; anyhow, she continued her course across the carpet. Embarrassed, shy, overwhelmed, I bend down to greet this creature. But the Professor says, "Do not touch her—she snaps—she is very difficult with strangers." *Strangers?* Is the Soul crossing the threshold, a stranger to the Door-Keeper? It appears so. But, though no accredited dog-lover, I like dogs and they oddly and sometimes unexpectedly "take" to me. If this is an exception, I am ready to take the risk. Unintimidated but distressed by the Professor's somewhat forbidding manner, I not only continue my gesture toward the little chow, but crouch on the floor so that she can snap better if she wants

to. Yofi—her name is Yofi—snuggles her
nose into my hand and nuzzles her head, in
delicate sympathy, against my shoulder.

76

SO AGAIN I can say the Professor was not
always right. That is, yes, he was always
right in his judgements, but my form of
rightness, my intuition, sometimes func-
tioned by the split-second (that makes all
the difference in spiritual time-computa-
tions) the quicker. I was swifter in some intuitive instances, and sometimes a small
tendril of a root from that great common
Tree of Knowledge went deeper into the
sub-soil. His were the great giant roots of
that tree, but mine, with hair-like almost
invisible feelers, sometimes quivered a warning or resolved a problem, as for instance
at the impact of that word *stranger*. "We'll
show him," retorts the invisible intuitive
rootlet; and, without forming the thought,
the words "love me, love my dog" are there
to prompt me. "He will see whether or not
I am indifferent," my *emotion* snaps back,
though not in words. "If he is so wise, so
clever," the smallest possible sub-soil rootlet

gives its message, "you show him that you too are wise, are clever. Show him that you have ways of finding out things about people, other than looking at their mere outward ordinary appearance." My intuition challenges the Professor, though not in words. That intuition can not really be translated into words, but if it could be it would go, roughly, something like this: "Why should I look at you? You are contained in the things you love, and if you accuse me of looking at the things in the room before looking at you, well, I will go on looking at the things in the room. One of them is this little golden dog. She snaps, does she? You call me a stranger, do you? Well, I will show you two things: one, I am not a stranger; two, even if I were, two seconds ago, I am now no longer one. And moreover I never was a stranger to this little golden Yofi."

The wordless challenge goes on, "You are a very great man. I am overwhelmed with embarrassment, I am shy and frightened and gauche as an over-grown school-girl. But listen. You are a man. Yofi is a dog. I am a woman. If this dog and this woman "take" to one another, it will prove that beyond your caustic implied criticism—if criticism it is—there is another region of cause and effect, another region of question and answer." Undoubtedly, the Professor took an important clue from the first reaction of a new analysand or patient. I was, as it happened, not prepared for this. It would have been worse for me if I had been.

77

"BY CHANCE OR intention," I started these notes on September 19th. Consulting my "Mysteries of the Ancients" calendar, I find Dr. W. B. Crow has assigned this date to "Thoth, Egyptian form of Mercury. Bearer of the Scales of Justice. *St. Januarius*." And we know of *Janus*, the old Roman guardian of gates and doors, patron of the month of January which was sacred to him, with all "beginnings."

Janus faced two ways, as doors and gates opened and shut. Here in this room, we had our exits and our entrances. I have noted too, the 4 sides of the room, and touched on the problem of the 4th dimensional: the "additional dimension attributed to space by a hypothetical speculation," is the somewhat comic dictionary definition. Old Janus was guardian of the seasons too, that time-sequence of the 4 quarters of the year. Thoth was the original measurer, the Egyptian prototype of the later Greek Hermes. I made the connecting link with the still later Roman Mercury, our Flying Dutchman.

For myself, there was a story I loved; I had completely "forgotten" it; now it is suddenly recalled. The story was about an old light-house keeper called Captain January and a ship-wrecked child.

We have only just begun our researches, our "studies," the old Professor and I.

78

THIS IS ONLY a beginning but I learned recently (again from Dr. Crow) that "the seal of the Hippocratic University bears the Tau-cross, entwined with the serpent— exactly the figure used by early Christian artists to represent the serpent which Moses lifted up in the wilderness." My serpent-and-thistle motif obviously bears some hidden relation to this.

It was Asklepios of the Greeks, who was called the *blameless physician*. He was the son of the sun, Phoebos Apollo, and music and medicine were alike sacred to this source of light. This half-man, half-god (Fate decreed) went a little too far when he began actually to raise the dead. He was blasted by the thunder-bolt of an avenging deity, but Apollo, over-riding his father's anger, placed Asklepios among the stars. Our Professor stood this side of the portal. He did not pretend to bring back the dead who had already crossed the threshold. But he raised from dead hearts and stricken minds and maladjusted bodies a host of living children.

One of these children was called Mignon. Not my name certainly. It is true I was small for my age, *mignonne;* but I was not, they said, pretty and I was not, it was very easy to see, quaint and quick and clever like my brother. My brother? Am I my brother's keeper? It appears so. A great many of these brothers fell on the fields of France, in that first war. A great many have fallen since. Numberless, poised, disciplined and valiant young winged Mercuries have fallen from the air, to join the great host of the dead. Leader of the Dead? That was Hermes of the Greeks who took the attribute from Thoth of the Egyptians. The *T* or Tau-cross became caduceus with twined serpents, again corresponding to the *T* or Tau-cross that Moses lifted in the desert.

Am I my brother's keeper? So far as my undisciplined thoughts permit me . . . and further than my disciplined ones can take me. For the Professor was not always right. He did not know—or did he?—that I looked at the things in his room before I looked at him; for I knew the things in his room were symbols of Eternity and contained him then, as Eternity contains him now.

79

THIS OLD JANUS, this beloved light-house keeper, old Captain January, shut the door on transcendental speculations or at least transferred this occult or hidden symbolism to the occult or hidden regions of the personal reactions, dreams, thought associations or thought "transferences" of the individual human mind. It was the human individual that concerned him, its individual reactions to the problems of every-day, the relation of the child to its environment, its friends, its teachers, above all its parents. As to what happened, after this life was over . . . we as individuals, we as members of one race, one brotherhood of body that contained many different, individual branches, had profited so little by the illuminating teaching of the Master who gave his name to our present era, that it was well for a Prophet, in the old tradition of Israel, to arise, to slam the door on visions of the future, of the after-life, to stand himself like the Roman Centurion before the gate at Pompeii, who did not move from his station before the gate-way since he had received no orders to do so, and who stood for later generations to wonder at, embalmed in hardened lava, preserved in the very fire and ashes that had destroyed him.

"At least, they have not burnt me at the stake." Did the Professor say that of himself or did someone else say it of him? I think he himself said it. But it was a near-miss . . . even literally . . . and last night, here in London, there were the familiar siren-shrieks, the alerts, each followed by its even more ear-piercing and soul-shattering "all-clear," which coming as a sort of aftermath or after-birth of the actual terror is the more devastating. Released from the threat of actual danger, we have time to think about it. And the "alerts" and the "all-clears" are punctuated by sound of near or far explosions, at 3 in the morning, after 7 and at lesser intervals . . . , the war is not yet over. *Eros* and *Death*, those two were the chief subjects—in fact, the only subjects—of the Professor's eternal pre-occupation. They are still gripped, struggling in the dead-lock. Hercules struggled with Death and is still struggling. But the Professor himself proclaimed the Herculean power of Eros and we know that it was written from the beginning that Love is stronger than Death.

It was the very love of humanity that caused the Professor to stand guardian at the gate. Belief in the soul's survival, in a life after death, wrote the Professor, was the last and greatest phantasy, the gigantic wish-fulfillment that had built up, through the ages, the elaborate and detailed picture of an after-life. He may even have believed this. If so, it was proof again of his Centurion courage. He would stand guardian, he would turn the whole stream of consciousness back into useful, into *irrigation* channels, so that none of this power be wasted. He would clean the Augean stables, he would tame the Nemean lion, he would capture the Erymanthian boar, he would clear the Stymphalian birds from the marshes of the unconscious mind. These things must be done. He indicated certain ways in which they might be done. Until we have completed our 12 labours, he seemed to reiterate, we (mankind) have no right to rest on cloud-cushion phantasies and dreams of an after-life.

From the reasoning upper layers of the thinking mind, he would shut off this dream of heaven, this hope of eternal life. Someone writes somewhere of Sigmund Freud's courageous pessimism. He had little hope for the world. He knew why people laughed at his first findings, at his *Interpretation of Dreams*, his *Delusion and Dream*, and the rest of them. He answered his first ribald detractors with his essay on wit and humour—I think it is impossible to assess this or appreciate it in the translation—but even a superficial observer of his manner of approach to his antagonists would have to grant that the foil of his wit, given a worthy adversary to measure it by, would have none to rival it. He did not wish to prove people *wrong*, he wanted only to show them the way and show them that others had imposed ideas on them that might eventually prove destructive. He even wrote a later, reasoned, calm and dispassionate essay on the causes for the re-surging hatred of the Jews.

THERE WAS another Jew who said, *the king-dom of heaven is within you.* He said: *unless you become as little children you shall not enter into the kingdom of heaven.*

Others abide our question. Thou art free.
We ask and ask—Thou smilest and art still,
Out-topping knowledge. For the loftiest hill,
Who to the stars uncrowns his majesty,

Planting his steadfast footsteps in the sea,
Making the heaven of heavens his dwelling-
      place,
Spares but the cloudy border of his base
To the foil'd searching of mortality;

'And thou, who didst the stars and sunbeams
      know,
Self-school'd, self-scann'd, self-honour'd, self-
      secure,
Didst tread on earth unguess'd at.—Better so!

All pains the immortal spirit must endure,
All weakness which impairs, all griefs which
  bow,
Find their sole speech in that victorious brow.

I was impelled (almost compelled) to copy this out. It is, of course, Matthew Arnold's familiar sonnet to Shakespeare. I had not intended to include it in these notes, but perhaps my subconscious or unconscious mind recognized an intellectual family-likeness in "that victorious brow." And in this very last line, there is a sort of Eliza-bethan conceit or posy, a hidden reference —a purely personal finding, but for our purpose curiously compelling. We have *victorious* or victory, *Sieg*, and the sole *voice*, the voice, or speech or utterance, *Mund*, Sigmund. There is this, this sonnet, as if written for us, for this occasion, for this memoir and there is the more personal lyric of the German poet, Goethe, to which I have referred earlier in these notes. I can not recall the musical setting—not Schu-mann's—that I and a group of my contem-poraries sang as school-children. But about the Professor, there was music certainly; there was music in every syllable he uttered and there was music implicit in his name, the *Sieg-mund*, the victorious voice or utterance. There had been music everywhere in Vienna, there was Beethoven, surcharged and tortured with his symphonies, Mozart, frail and impeccable and deserted and early dead. There was Schumann, of course, and Schubert's name was especially associated with the village or suburb of Grinzig, not far from Döbling where the Professor had his summer-quarters that first year I was in Vienna. There was the city acclaimed by the world as the heart and centre of music and music-lovers. And here was the master-musician, he, too, a son of Apollo, who would harmonize the whole human spirit, who like Orpheus, would charm the very beasts of the unconscious or subconscious mind, and enliven the dead sticks and stones of buried thoughts and memories.

82

"BY CHANCE OR intention," I began these notes on September 19th, a day sacred to Thoth and later to St. Januarius, a name affiliated with that of the Roman Janus, patron of gate-ways and portals, guardian of all "beginnings." I did not consciously select this date, though, as I glance at the

Calendar from time to time, my subconscious mind might have guided me to it. But by quite definite "intention," I will finish these "beginnings," as for November 2nd, the day of the lighting of candles for the souls of the Dead.

This is the evening of All Hallows, hallow-e'en; so tomorrow is the first of November, 1944, All Saints Day. The angel Michael of the old dispensation, the archangel Michael of the Revelation, is regent of the planet still called Mercury. And in Renaissance paintings, we are not surprised to see Saint Michael wearing the winged sandals and sometimes even the winged helmet of the classic messenger of the Gods. But for the Professor, I choose rather the day following All Saints Day. He was more interested in souls than saints.

83

ONE OF THESE souls was called Mignon, though its body did not fit it very well. It was small, *mignonne*, though it was not pretty, they said. It was a girl between two boys; but, ironically, it was wispy and mousey, while the boys were glowing and gold. It was not pretty, they said. Then they said it was pretty—but suddenly, it shot up like a weed. They said, surprised, "She is really very pretty, but isn't it a pity she's so tall?" The soul was called Mignon, but, clearly, it did not fit its body.

But it found itself in a song. Only the tune is missing.

84

IN THE LAST verse of this lyric of Johann Wolfgang Goethe is the line,

Es stürzt der Fels,

the rock breaks or falls in ruins, and indeed this is our very present predicament; but

und über ihn die Flut

following, gives the impression of a living river; though "and over it the flood," is the literal rendering. Ruins and the flood, but there remains our particular Ark or Barque —a canoe, I called it—that may, even yet, carry us through the seething channels to safe harbour. The Mignon of Goethe's lyric herself joins us in our ritual of question and answer. There were the question-marks, as

I called them, the series of the imperfect, reversed *S* of the scroll-pattern of the writing-on-the-wall in the Greek island of Corfu, in the spring of the year, 1920. There was the *S* or the serpent of my original corner-stone, the enigmatic symbol that a childhood friend, my first "live" poet, Ezra Pound, translated for me. There was the *S* as serpent, companion to the thistle, the symbol that suggests waste places and the desert; but we have been told that *the desert shall blossom as the rose*, and it was in the desert that Moses raised the standard, the old *T* or Tau-cross of Thoth of the Egyptians. The Professor had been working on a continuation of his "Moses, the Egyptian" theme, though we had not actually discussed this when I had my "real" dream of the Egyptian Princess. The Professor asked me then, if I were the child Miriam who in the Doré picture had stood, half-hidden in the river-reeds, watching over the new-born child who was to become leader of a captive people and founder of a new religion. Miriam? Mignon?

85

SHE ASKS THE question. Each verse of the lyric is a question or a series of questions. Do you know the Land? Do you know the House? Do you know the Mountain?

Kennst du den Berg und seinen Wolkensteg?

"Do you know the mountain and its cloud-bridge" is an awkward enough translation but the idea of mountain and bridge is so very suitable to this whole *translation* of the Professor and our work together. *Steg* really means a plank; *foot-bridge* is the more accurate rendering. It is not a bridge for a great crowd of people, and it is a bridge flung, as it were, across the abyss, not built and hammered and constructed. There is plenty of psycho-analytic building and constructing; there are the Gods that some people read Goods. We are dealing here with the realm of phantasy and imagination, flung across the abyss, and these are a poet's lines. The same poet's following lines seem peculiarly appropriate to our subject:

Das Maultier sucht im Nebel seinen Weg,

"The donkey seeks his way in the mist." There are plenty of donkeys who have set foot on the lower, more easily demarked path-ways of this mountain. Too heavily burdened with intellectual equipment or blinded with the blinkers of prejudice, they go round and round in circles and come back to the stable shaking their heads sadly over their own past folly and the greater folly of the mountain that has so beguiled them. But there are other donkeys who plod on—faithful donkeys. They find their proto-type in the Christmas manger-scene.

And our very Phobia is here and the host of allied Phobias, the Dragon and its swarm of children, the Hydra-headed monster, the subject of another of the 12 labours of Hercules.

In Höhlen wohnt der Drachen alte Brut,

the old dragon-brood—or the ancient brood of the Dragon—lives in the caves. Like the Christian of the Puritan poet, John Bunyan, we must push on, through and past these perils. *Kennst du ihn wohl?* Do you actually know this and all these things? If anyone ever did, it is the old Professor. And it was finally St. Michael—wasn't it?—who cast out that aboriginal old Beast? Thoth, Hermes, Mercury, and last Michael, Captain or Centurion of the hosts of heaven.

But it is with the soul rather than with

saints and angels that we are concerned; Miriam or Mignon, we may call her.

Kennst du das Land, wo die Zitronen blühn?

"Do you know the land where the orange-tree blossoms?" It was on a winter day that the Professor handed me a branch from an orange-tree with dark laurel-like leaves.

Im dunkeln Laub die Gold-Orangen glühn.

Against the dark leaves is that glow of orange-gold.

Ein sanfter Wind vom blauen Himmel weht;

yes, it was dark and cold and there was the rumbling of war-chariots from the near horizon. But upon the old Professor and this particular soul, a soft wind blew from a cloudless sky—so gentle was the wind that the myrtle, that with the rose is sacred to Love, did not flutter a leaf, and the laurel grew very tall there.

Die Myrte still und hoch der Lorbeer steht.

It is all there; the lyrical interrogation and the implication that the answer is given with it. It is: do you know the Land—but you do know it, don't you? The House? The Mountain? It is a strange land, a foreign land, a land of classic associations, the myrtle of Aphrodite and the laurel of Apollo. You do know the House, don't you? The roof of the house stood on pillars, like the original roof or part-roof of the temple of Karnak or the Parthenon of Athens. But this house seems nearer in time; there is the great entrance-room or *Saal* with its glowing lamps and candles, and beyond it is the brightly tapestried or painted inner-room or rooms, the *Gemach* or apartment. It is there that we find the statues, the *Marmorbilder*, even as I had found the little images in the room beyond the actual consulting room, on the Professor's table. The statues stare and stare and seem to say, what has happened to you?

Was hat man dir, du armes Kind, getan?

Poor child, poor shivering and unprotected soul. But—you do know it?—but of course you do. I want to go there with you, O my Guardian (O my Protector),

mit dir, o mein Beschützer, ziehn.

The land or country, the house, the mountain—we may rest in the garden, we may be sheltered within that house; it is so beautiful; it makes me think of the *Ca d'Oro*, the Golden House on the Grand Canal in Venice. It is the *domus aurea* of the Laurentian litany, and the whole poem in its symbolism follows the cycle of the soul's progress. The garden, the house or hall, the mountain. The mountain is very high for it is crowned like Olympus with clouds, but there is the *Wolkensteg*, the cloud-bridge or foot-way. It is not a very wide bridge, the chasms or gulfs where the ancient dragon lives are deep and terrifying. (But *we have tunnelled very deep*, said the old Professor.) Scattered rocks and ruins lie about us and the threatening roar of the cataract is still echoing in our ears. But you, of all people, know it, don't you, the inquiring soul asks; while the plodding little donkey continues its way in the mist. O, let's go away together, pleads the soul, the Mignon of the poet Goethe; let's go, O my dearest, she says first,

o mein Geliebter,

then O my guardian, my protector,

o mein Beschützer,

and in the end, she does not ask if she may go; or exclaim, if only we could go; but there is the simple affirmation, with the white roses—or the still whiter gardenias, as it happened—of uttermost veneration.

Dahin! Dahin
Geht unser Weg! o Vater, lass uns ziehn!

London
September 19, 1944
November 2, 1944

APPENDIX

Reading the letters from Freud to H. D., one early-winter's day in Switzerland where she now lives, it was clear to me that they properly belonged in an appendix to her homage to "the Professor." Not as affidavit, but as an extension of that companionable warmth which Freud extended toward the creative spirit and its search for identity and direction.

So I asked H. D. for the privilege of printing the letters here, and then, later, secured permission from his heirs for those which they selected from the number he had written her. Of these nine letters which they chose, the ones dated June 26, 1933; July 20, 1933; December 28, 1935; May 1936; September 20, 1936, and February 26, 1937 were written in German and are printed in a translation by Annemarie Holborn. The others are in Freud's own English. All of these letters in the appendix, published for the first time, are included "By Permission of Sigmund Freud Copyrights Ltd."

N.H.P.

Dec. 18th. 1932
Wien IX., Berggasse 19

Dear Mrs. Aldington

I am not sure of your knowing German so I beg to accept my bad English. It may be especially trying to a poet.

You will understand that I did not ask for your books in order to criticise or to appreciate your work, which I have been informed is highly praised by your readers. I am a bad judge on poetry especially in a foreign language. I wanted to get a glimpse of your personality as an introduction to making your personal acquaintance. Your books will be waiting with me for your arrival. (An american friend of mine brought me today "Palimpsest".)

My relations to my patients (or pupils) are now especially complicated. I hope to arrange them in a few weeks and I will make an effort not to let you stay in waiting very long.

With kind regards
yours sincerely
Freud

Dear Madam

I did not answer the charming letter you wrote to me late in December. At that time I hoped to be able to call you here very soon. But things have turned out differently. I did not succeed in finding time for you and kept postponing a decision. Now your second letter has reached me, together with the book on H. Ellis, which shall wait here for your arrival. I understand that a certain delay was quite agreeable to you. But I do not want to extend it too long, and I have made up my mind to make the necessary arrangements, even if it means using force. On the other hand, I cannot expect you to travel or change your place of residence in this present biting cold and at a time when an epidemic of grippe is spreading. I have heard that you are of delicate health. Would you prefer to come at the beginning of spring, in April/May? It is hard to control these hygienic factors and easy to make miscalculations.

Sachs wrote about you and your friends from Boston. I have not heard from H. Ellis— I owned already the book in honor of his 70th birthday and have taken note of who is meant by the lofty person of the revelation.

With kindest regards to you and your friends,

Yours,
Freud

P.S. *Glad you understand German.*

20 July 1933
Wien IX., Berggasse 19

Dear H. D.

Thank you for your long letter which was written under such sad circumstances. I have already had a letter from Bryher from London. Probably the future depends on how Lady E. will feel. I talked to Yo and Tattoun: "You careless pack, you do not realize that Sir John is dead and that you may never have Perdita as your foster-mother nor see Villa Kenwin." Since you have to part with them and this parting is very hard on you, you wish at least to see them in good hands. There has been much commotion in the dog-state. Wolf had to be shipped off to Kagran, because both ladies were in heat, and the fierce antagonism between Yofi and Lün, which is rooted in the nature of women, resulted in good, gentle Lün's being bitten by Yofi. Thus Lün, too, is at present in Kagran and her future is uncertain.

*About the human occupants of the house
I can only report that they have been ill much
of the time and only now begin to enjoy the
summer.*

*I confidently expected to hear from you
that you are writing, but such matter should
never be forced. I trust I shall hear so later on.*

*The Spanish adventure about which you re-
port is terrible and mysterious. . . .*

With kindest regards,
Yours,
Freud

March 5th 1934
Wien IX., Berggasse 19

Dear H. D.!
  *Is it really a whole year since you first called
on me? Yes, and the second half of this term
I spent in suffering owing to the bad effects
of another slight operation which was intended
to relieve my habitual ailings. But after all it
was not a tragic affair, only the inevitable expression of old age and the degeneration of
tissues dependent on it. So I do not complain.
I know I am overdue and whatever I still have
is an unexpected gift.*

  Nor is it too painful a thought to leave this

scene and set of phenomena for good. There is not much left to be regretted, times are cruel and the future appears to be disastrous. For a while we were afraid we will not be able to stay in this town and country—it is unpleasant to go into exile at the age of 78—but now we think we have escaped at least this danger.

We passed through a week of civil war. Not much personal suffering, just one day without electric light, but the "stimmung" was awful and the feeling as of an earthquake. No doubt, the rebels belonged to the best portion of the population, but their success would have been very shortlived and brought about military invasion of the country. Besides they were Bolshevists and I expect no salvation from Communism. So we could not give our sympathy to either side of the combatants.

I am sorry to hear you do not yet work but according to your own account the forces are seething. From Perdita's trip, I am getting postcards. The last came from Trinidad. Happy girl!

Give my love to Bryher and don't forget me.

Yours affectionately
Freud

Dear H. D. and Perdita:

I think I shall prefer to continue in German. We here, too, have more fog and darkness than is usual around Christmastime. But in front of my window in the inner room stands a proud, sweet-smelling plant. Only twice have I seen it in bloom in a garden, at the Lago di Garda and in the Val Lugano. It reminds me of those bygone days when I was still able to move around and visit the sunshine and beauty of southern nature myself. It is a datura, a noble relative of the tobacco plant, whose leaves used to do so much for me in former times but now can do so little.

It is hardly advisable to give an octogenarian something beautiful. There is too much sadness mixed in with the enjoyment. But one thing is certain: I have not deserved this gift from you and Perdita, since I did not even answer your friendly letters regularly.

I sincerely return your kind wishes for a good year 1936. You, and especially Perdita, still have so much ahead of you. I hope there will be much that is good and liberating. Also Bryher must allow me to thank her at least in this connection.

In warm friendship,

yours,
Freud

MY SINCERE THANKS FOR YOUR KIND
REMEMBRANCE ON THE OBSERVANCE
OF MY EIGHTIETH BIRTHDAY

Your Freud

*Will you forgive me this barbaric reaction
to such loving expressions [of friendship]? I
am sure Yofi is very proud of being mentioned
by you. Believe it or not, early on the 6th she
came into my bedroom to show me her affection in her own fashion, something she has
never done before or after. How does a little
animal know when a birthday comes around?*

[24 May 1936]
XIX Strasserg 47
Wien IX., Berggasse 19

Dear H. D.
*All your white cattle safely arrived lived
and adorned the room up to yesterday.*
*I had imagined I had become insensitive to
praise and blame. Reading your kind lines and
getting aware of how I enjoyed them I first
thought I had been mistaken about my firm-
ness. Yet on second thoughts I concluded I
was not. What you gave me, was not praise,*

was affection and I need not be ashamed of my satisfaction.

Life at my age is not easy, but spring is beautiful and so is love.

Yours affectionately
Freud

20 September 1936
Wien IX., Berggasse 19

Belated, though sincere, congratulations on the occasion of your fiftieth birthday from an 80 year-old friend.

Fr.

26 February 1937
Wien IX., Berggasse 19

Dear H. D.

I have just finished your Ion. *Deeply moved by the play (which I had not known before) and no less by your comments, especially those referring to the end, where you extol the victory of reason over passions, I send you the expression of my admiration and kindest regards,*

Yours,
Freud